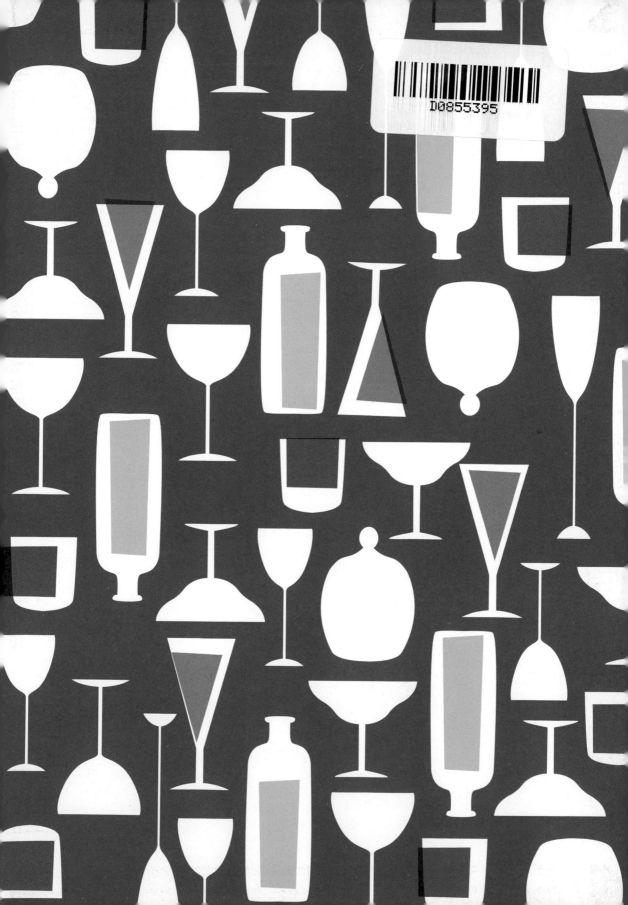

Tony Conigliaro is a revolutionary. He is at the forefront of a new energy in cocktail making. His research is exhaustive and his commitment has resulted in some delicious and innovative cocktails.

His inspiration comes from such diverse extremes as movies and perfumes and his knowledge of alcohol history dates back to alchemy itself. He has a great insight into the spirits and the alcohol he uses and the various processes of their creation. This solid foundation of knowledge is the building block for his creativity. His respect and understanding of the produce he uses in his drinks result in delicious, intense flavors as he pushes the rules of classic cocktail making beyond expectation.

Tony's enthusiasm does not just stop with the drink in the glass. He is concerned with every component, from the presentation, color, smell, type of receptacle used, to the way in which the ice is frozen and its effects on taste and flavor. By using modern equipment not normally associated with the tools of a cocktail barman, Tony manages to extract the best possible flavors from his marinades and infusions, resulting in a cleaner, sharper quality of cocktail. His commitment to research and development is a breath of fresh air, and he has a strong focus on reinventing iconic classics.

With the publication of the recipes in *The Cocktail Lab*, the skill and enthusiasm that Tony brings to the industry, combined with his pure raw energy, will help the enthusiast to unfold the mysteries surrounding his philosophy and approach to cocktail making—and maybe trigger a few ideas of their own.

HESTON BLUMENTHAL

The COCKTAIL LAB

Tony Conigliaro ————————

TEN SPEED PRESS
Berkeley

For my mentors Richard "Dick" Bradsell, Rainer "ja ja" Becker for believing in me, and my dear friend Audrey "smell this" Saunders, for all the incredible walks and talks.

And for Ria "my Lighting Bolt" Soler, well, for being the lighting bolt.

Last but not least, Gemma "you're driving me mad" Reeves, without whom this book would not be possible.

Contents

I.
INTRODUCTION

In The Beginning There Was Art

There's a beginning to every story. This story begins in a white box-room with a sink, a rickety secondhand chair, an easel, and a table—the top of which was piled with bills. It was in this room that I discovered that supporting yourself *after* art school is as challenging as life *at* art school! After studying fine art and art history in London, I specialized in painting and experimented with using aroma in paint. In this sense, I've always been interested in working in one arena but exchanging ideas with an entirely different discipline. More from necessity than anything else, I began working in the bar industry—quite simply, I needed to fund my studio work. The crossover between the two disciplines was truly surprising. I had no idea of the creativity involved in working with cocktails. The two passions overlapped and then slowly one overtook the other. And so my love affair with liquids began.

Although art and cocktails seem to be disparate disciplines, they are both about appealing to sensory experience. At art school I read a lot about the philosophy of aesthetics and I asked myself questions all the time: why does one thing appeal to the senses over another, or appeal to just one of our senses rather than all? I think that there is real beauty in simplicity, in functionality. Cocktails are often talked about with a lack of sentimentality, yet many find it easy to become rapturous over wine. When I began to work in the bar industry the focus started to shift. I wondered: why is flavor in liquids beautiful?

6

And Then There Was Flavor

When we ask questions about flavor, our natural response is to turn to the culinary experience as a frame of reference. I love to cook and I revel in the dining experience. Growing up in a Sicilian family, I've always been surrounded with simple, flavor-packed home cooking. I taste dishes over and over again, comparing similar flavors, using the same ingredients with different variations. One of my favorite dishes to cook at home is wild mushroom risotto. Over the years I've honed the recipe to perfection and this is because the devil really is in the detail. Each element of the risotto is important; it's about using just the right amount of stock, the quality and variety of the mushrooms, and I replace white wine with dry vermouth for a lovely nutty flavor. The enjoyment of the finished dish is dependent upon all these small details working in harmony to achieve the perfect final texture.

In fact, much of what we enjoy about food is centered around texture and chewing, but with liquids the mechanism of how you taste is different. People tend to think that taste is just flavor on the tongue, but in actuality the salty/sweet/sour aspects of flavor are also like touch—a sensation, not just a flavor in themselves. Flavor is only really released when you swallow something. At the back of your palate is the epiglottis, which is open when you breathe; when you swallow, it closes so that the liquid doesn't flow down into your airways. When it reopens, it releases a reflux of aroma molecules back into the olfactory chamber—so when you're tasting something, you're really smelling it. Therefore, the majority of taste is smell, and this is also why the way in which we enjoy cocktails can have much in common with how we enjoy perfumes as well as food.

For this reason, when it comes to liquids there is little or no distraction of texture, of masticating—no knife, no fork. Alcohol can be a fantastic vehicle for delivering immediate flavor. In this sense we are slaves to the first few seconds of taste and it is in those moments that we'll decide whether or not we like a cocktail; our decision whether we love or loathe a drink is rarely an afterthought—the flavor may keep on developing in our mouth, but it wins or loses at that first point. There's a huge challenge in this: to fulfill a person's sensory experience immediately!

Cocktails are a niche market and they inhabit a nebulous space. They don't sit comfortably in the food category, but because they are ingested rather than inhaled it doesn't feel right to consider them in the same spectrum as perfume either. Part of understanding the beauty in liquid flavor comes from trying to find a language that expresses working with liquids for liquid's sake. One of the first steps in creating your own language is to borrow the terminology and signifiers, and when talking about cocktails it makes sense to turn to cocktail historians, perfumers, and chefs. Challenging the traditional approach to working with alcohol and the language we use to discuss it is no easy feat. Talking about how booze makes you feel is almost a taboo subject—essentially we are discussing the effects of a drug, so how can this be art—how can this be beautiful? People will drink alcohol whether or not it tastes good; we don't grow up drinking alcoholic drinks—we haven't spent a lifetime drinking in the same way that we have eating. And so we have to educate our palates much later in life. I think, however, that there is an inherent sense of artistry in drink because of its frivolity—you don't need to have a Bellini, but it's a damn good feeling when you do.

Studying the Structure

Drinks are by no means universally delicious but there are solid reasons why some just taste better than others. To make a truly delicious cocktail you have to triumph over flavor—manipulate it, have a command over it—and the only way to achieve this is to understand its structure. So I often pull the different components of the cocktail apart, study them separately, and then put the cocktail back together in the way that I want it. I've spent years studying the structure of drink in this manner, not just reading and researching, but experimenting, testing a formula and pushing its boundaries. If you sample a Dry Martini in twenty or thirty different ways, then you simply have a better insight than you would merely trusting theories and reading recipes. Bartending is a craft.

The passion and dedication that I put into each cocktail can span months, and on occasion, even years. I don't believe in cobbling stuff together. I refine things, test things, make them a hundred times over to push the limits until I achieve exactly what I set out to. It's important not simply to accept the first result; there are usually more interesting findings sitting just behind it. I always tinker with the projects that I'm working on, as well as revisit old projects because there is always a new way of doing things. Every recipe has space to be refreshed, to be renewed, over time. It's true of anything: the more energy you put into something, the better the product.

The linchpin of this approach to drinks is the Drink Factory consultancy, a research and development company that I founded in 2005. Now housed in Pink Floyd's old recording studios, the Drink Factory has its own laboratory—the first of its kind in the U.K., focusing as it does entirely on alcohol-development and research into liquid flavor. Home to sophisticated lab machinery such as the centrifuge and Rotavapor, the lab functions to produce bespoke ingredients and develop new recipes. With clients as diverse as chefs, perfume houses, chocolatiers, and soft drinks companies, an ordinary day in the lab can involve thermo-mixing, sous-viding, dehydrating—even stripping bark from trees!

The collection of equipment housed at the laboratory is nothing sort of esoteric, but each piece of machinery shares the same goal—to match the level of accuracy and innovation of ideas and flavor combinations that chefs worldwide are able to achieve, but to translate this knowledge from the kitchen to the bar world. It's not about being niche; rather, it's about reaching for the unimagined, to create new combinations, to appeal to all five senses, as well as the sixth sense—instinct. The equipment in the lab quantifies what I aim to do intuitively. Throughout this book the measurements of ingredients vary from grams to milliliters and microliters ($^1/_{1000}$ of a milliliter). Although this may seem unusual, it is a deliberate move with a view toward total accuracy at all times. When making individual cocktails I always use a jigger to measure each component to ensure that the drink is made exactly the same each time. The same approach goes for pre-preparing or making ingredients in batches, which often involves measuring in a mixture of grams and milliliters. In this way, cocktails are all about emotional functionality—to make something repeatedly wonderful.

Here would be a good place to discuss the U.S. edition of *The Cocktail Lab*. Most of the recipes in this book have been Americanized, with ounce measurements added, in parentheses, to the ingredients lists. The goal was to make these recipes accessible to U.S. readers, many of whom do not own a jigger with metric measurements. It's worth noting that many of the recipes call for $^1/_3$- or $^2/_3$-ounce pours, so if you are using the U.S. measurement conversions, I recommend you buy a jigger with $^1/_3$-ounce increments. Some of the recipes do not have American conversions at all, simply because the measurements are too small to be converted into nonmetric—a microliter or tenth of a gram, for instance. However, these recipes require the use of a micropipette or digital scale, both of which will display units in metric.

Over the years I have worked at numerous bars including Isola and the Shochu Lounge, all of which were instrumental in developing my approach to drinks. The real turning point for me, however, was in 2009 when I opened my own venue, 69 Colebrooke Row, in Islington, North London. The bar was designed as a 1950s-style Italian café with film noir touches, while retaining a "living-room" feel to encourage an intimate, friendly atmosphere.

The menu at Colebrooke Row is deceptively simple: twelve cocktails with minimal descriptors, three wines and champagnes, and just one beer. Without prior knowledge customers have no idea just how much work goes into creating the bespoke ingredients used in their cocktails. I like to keep the science and processes out of the customer's direct experience; bartending isn't simply about the drinks—it's as much about hosting and high levels of service. Those customers who do want to know more tend to ask. I like the idea that the rest will contentedly sip on a Bloody Mary, blissfully unaware that it took two years to perfect each individual component of their drink.

History and Mythology

Technology is an extremely important means of progression. However, it's not the sole focus of my drinks. The world of cocktails is rich in history, and coming from a background in art history, I simply extended my learning. However, a lot of cocktail history remains impenetrable and it can be very hard to distinguish the truth from mythology. I think this can be an asset! While recognizing that deconstructing cocktail history is part of learning to be analytic and understanding why things work, fantasy and mythology have their merits too, and what I love about this duality is that it can be utilized for the benefit of the cocktail experience. Playing upon mythology means that we can create a refuge or suspension from reality—which is exactly what drinking and bars are about. You go to a bar to get away from the craziness of everyday life. Part of the psychology of drinking is to separate a piece of yourself from the whole. I love the look on a customer's face when I explain exactly how their seemingly simple-looking Bloody Mary actually came together. It's as if you can create a stage and all the flavors and characters have to dance around and play their parts within it. Like telling ghost stories around the campfire, I start the first paragraph of the story and the customer defines the next. They may tell a friend about their experience in the bar and that person subsequently writes the following chapter.

I'm often asked whether I believe that we are living in a second golden age of cocktails. Years ago it was a struggle to find good cocktail books, but now there is an abundance of information; the Internet is buzzing, alive with blogs and foodie websites, and there are bar shows all over the world. This flow of information is incredible and it stimulates a lot of discourse around cocktails. It's completely different from the first golden age of cocktails because there was so much less out there. If you are lucky enough to talk to people from that era, they trained and they read what was available—cocktail knowledge was far more obtuse.

The cocktail world is indeed changing. In the past fifteen to twenty years, the bartending world has evolved and it continues to do so. Bartenders exercise their expertise not just through the medium of what has come before them, but rather they are a generation that wants to put its own mark on drinks. As the industry has grown, it has become more creative. The modern bartender is all about creating his or her own style; you go to see particular people for their personal styles of drinks, just as you would chefs. Attitudes toward drink are also changing. The way people appreciate food and drink nowadays has changed dramatically. It's not simply the bartenders who have worked really hard toward this, but the drinks community as a whole who have pushed the boundaries of what people drink. Customers are more demanding—they know more about drinks, and it's important that we feed that enthusiasm.

"The Cocktail Lab"

The recipes in this book demonstrate the different styles that I have worked in: the simple, the difficult, and the stuff in between. The first five chapters naturally developed their own characters, and it wasn't until I started to revisit old recipes that they began to evolve into quite distinct areas of interest. I found that the drinks shared a genealogy—an idea was born, then pushed, then pushed further, changing slightly and then being changed again. I would look at the ingredients of a cocktail one way and then this would open up a new line of thinking—a chain reaction—just like my initial involvement in the cocktail industry.

New cocktails are usually born from experimenting with flavor connections and listening to a gut instinct. The recipes in this book are often quite romantic in nature. Yes, they have historical references, but they go beyond that. Inspiration can come from many places, not always obviously related to cocktails, and they straddle diverse terrains—from perfume to films, from poetry to an image of a landscape. Others were inspired by well-loved regulars at my bars—characters worthy of a book in themselves! These stories imbue a hint of fantasy to otherwise quite technical products. I have to be very thankful for my distractions!

When I said earlier that cocktails occupy a nebulous place, so too does this book. It is not a classic cocktail book, nor is it a bar manual. There are recipes here for the home enthusiast but also for the technician. Some of the recipes are known or have solid references, but here my aim is to demonstrate there can be a new point of interest or perspective—what inspired them, how they came together, how they've changed, and why they work. Consider it a guide to liquid flavor...

1.
CLASSICS
& SPINS

Classics & Spins

There are but a handful of cocktails that become survivors of history; more often than not, cocktail recipes are history's victims. The past few years have seen a revival in sourcing classic cocktail recipes and making them to their exact original specification. This resurgence has helped us to develop a cultural and social understanding of that cocktail's epoch, which can tell us as much about the bartender who was making it as the person who consumed it.

Everything has a genealogy that links it to the past, and the classics are important for learning our trade, to understand structure, techniques, and how flavors work. However, adhering to a blind belief in classic drinks is to negate the extraordinary hard work of the modern bartender and modern times. Too often we have been guilty of being dismissive of the new and sticking with the security of the classics. This argument was more valid when we bartenders were unsure of ourselves and our trade. But I now believe that the idea is to keep pushing the boundaries and combinations until something sticks—this is how modern classics are born.

For me, one of the most exciting aspects of discovering classic recipes is to modernize them—to find a way to make them work so that they are more accessible or acceptable to the modern palate. As the cocktail enthusiast David Embury once so poignantly acknowledged, cocktails work around basic structures. But if you start playing with each component—taking one out, putting one in and exchanging it—then that structure starts to waver somewhat. The drink does not have to be clearly defined; you can shift things slightly.

What's new is old and what's old is new. It's how you approach the old that makes it new—how you bring things back to life. Otherwise, these drinks become lost in cocktail books, hidden away from the general public. Learning and growing, alongside technological advances, have made revisiting traditional, simple cocktail recipes an interesting and unique experience. I really enjoy taking a recipe that is two hundred years old and applying modern processes, which can result in a slicker, more flavorful, and more direct drink. Recipes evolve, as do palates, and consequently we must keep abreast of that evolution.

During the fifteen years that I have been working in the industry, I have made the same classic cocktail in countless different ways. The following chapter showcases my tried-and-tested classic cocktail recipes, a lot of which are the drinks that I most like to consume! The recipes that follow them are the "spins"—the drinks that I went on to create, which were inspired by their predecessors but took their flavor profile and waltzed them off into a new direction.

For me, one of the most exciting aspects of discovering classic recipes is to modernize them—to find a way to make them work so that they are more accessible or acceptable to the modern palate.

Buck's Fizz

1. Pour the juice into a cocktail tin and follow with the champagne.

2. Stir slowly with a bar spoon before pouring into a champagne flute.

INGREDIENTS
— 25 ml (^{3}/$_4$ oz) fresh orange juice
— 100 ml (3 oz) champagne

Clementine Buck's Fizz ^{2007}

This version of the Buck's Fizz uses freshly pressed organic clementine juice for its sweet, floral taste, which complements the acidity of the orange juice. However, it is using a homogenizer that really sets this drink apart from other Buck's Fizzes. The oils from the zest stretch the citrus flavor further by providing a slight bitterness—a flavor that usually reaches the palate last, as bitter chemicals are bigger and take longer to get inside the mouth. The job of our saliva is to break down the size of particles in order to taste them, but a homogenizer breaks down all the filaments and walls of the zest for us, dividing them into small particles. This makes the taste process more immediate and fulfilling.

Getting the balance right in this drink took a while because the acidity levels of the fruit must work in harmony with those of the champagne. This Buck's Fizz is a perfect example of how simple drinks often require only small adjustments to transform them into something truly outstanding.

1. Pour the juice mix into a cocktail tin and follow with the champagne.

2. Stir slowly with a bar spoon before pouring into a champagne flute or coupette.

INGREDIENTS
— 25 ml (^{3}/$_4$ oz) homogenized orange and clementine juice (page 163)
— 100 ml (3 oz) champagne

Pink Grapefruit Buck's Fizz ²⁰¹⁰

1. Pour the juice into a cocktail tin and follow with the champagne.

2. Stir slowly with a bar spoon before pouring into a champagne flute or coupette.

INGREDIENTS
— 25 ml (¾ oz) homogenized pink grapefruit juice (page 163)
— 100 ml (3 oz) champagne

Clementine Buck's Fizz

Death in Venice

Sbagliato

1. Build the Campari and vermouth in a rocks glass over cubed ice. Stir and top with the Prosecco.

2. Stir again and garnish with a slice of orange.

INGREDIENTS
— 25 ml ($^3/_4$ oz) Campari
— 25 ml ($^3/_4$ oz) sweet vermouth
— 75 ml ($2^1/_4$ oz) Prosecco
— Orange slice, to garnish

Death in Venice ^{2010}

I have always liked Italy's concept of the *aperitivo* hour. A stopgap between lunch and late dinner, when you can enjoy an aperitif-style drink—whether it be a Negroni, Sbagliato, or Spritz—it becomes a real social event and a civilized way to unwind from work and begin the evening. My business partner, Camille, loves Campari, Spritzers, and Venice. This drink, as well as being an ode to the aperitif, is my ode to her and her liquid loves.

The Sbagliato was the launchpad for this drink, but I was after a lighter cocktail that could mirror its complexities while being as refreshing as a Spritz. The result was a cocktail that carefully pivots on a complex interplay between Campari, with its heavily bitter orange flavor, zesty dry grapefruit bitters, and Prosecco. A small orange twist completes the layering of multidimensional touches that harmonize bitterness, dryness, and citrus for a fresh and lively finish. Served in a champagne flute, this drink packs in far more flavor than just an ordinary Spritz.

1. Pour the Campari into a champagne flute.

2. Add three dashes of homemade grapefruit bitters and top with the Prosecco.

3. Stir gently. Finish with a small twist of orange.

INGREDIENTS
— 15 ml ($^1/_2$ oz) Campari
— 3 dashes of homemade grapefruit bitters (page 192)
— 125 ml ($4^1/_4$ oz) Prosecco
— Orange twist (page 221), to finish

White Gin Fizz

Silver Gin Fizz

1. Combine the gin, lemon juice, sugar syrup, and egg white in a cocktail tin.

2. Dry shake and shake again over cubed ice. Strain into a highball glass with one cube of ice in it, top with soda water, and gently stir.

INGREDIENTS
— 35 ml ($1^1/_4$ oz) gin
— 20 ml ($^2/_3$ oz) fresh
   lemon juice
— 15 ml ($^1/_2$ oz) sugar syrup
— 20 ml ($^2/_3$ oz) egg white
— Soda water, to top

White Gin Fizz ²⁰⁰⁰

I find the classic Silver Gin Fizz, which uses egg white, to be slightly oily and often egg-heavy. I was looking for the same sherbet taste but with a real fizz finish. The sorbet provides the same effect that egg white does but is lighter and smoother. This simple modification of one ingredient in an already fantastic recipe results in a perfectly balanced and refreshing fizz.

1. Shake all the ingredients except for the soda and orange slice in a cocktail tin and strain into a highball or rocks glass.

2. Top with soda water and gently stir. Garnish with an orange slice.

INGREDIENTS
— 50 ml ($1^1/_2$ oz) gin
— 25 ml ($^3/_4$ oz) fresh
   lemon juice
— 10 ml (2 tsp) sugar syrup
— 1 scoop of homemade
   lemon sorbet (page 209)
— Soda water, to top
— Orange slice, to garnish

Sgroppino

1. Combine all the ingredients in a blender and blend briefly.

2. Pour into a hurricane glass.

The Cocktail Lab | 22 | Tony Conigliaro

INGREDIENTS
— 20 ml ($^2/_3$ oz) vodka
— 2 scoops of lemon
  ice cream
— 75 ml ($2^1/_2$ oz)
  champagne or Prosecco

Elegante [1999]

One of the most interesting elements of taste is how it can trigger memories. For me, summers spent in Sicily are synonymous with drinking Sgroppino. When creating the original menu at Isola in 1999, the Elegante arose from my desire for an elegant blended drink, as those were getting a panning at the time. Inspired by the summery Sgroppino, I decided to make a more refined and refreshing version.

I began by making sorbet and playing with the proportions of vodka. By exchanging the creaminess of ice cream for sorbet and blending the Prosecco, the bubbles break but keep their fizz, and this combination makes for a delicious sherbet tang. Over the last decade it has been both a summer favorite and a drink that can be tailored according to the seasons. I have also adapted the recipe with homemade mandarin and raspberry sorbets, both of which add a new dimension to the cocktail.

1. Place all the ingredients except for the lemon in a blender and blend for approximately 30 seconds—a smooth sound indicates that the ice chips are ground.

2. Pour the mix into a coupette and finish by using the small holes of a citrus zester to express the oils from the lemon's zest over the drink.

INGREDIENTS
— 50 ml ($1^1/_2$ oz) vodka
— 25 ml ($^3/_4$ oz) fresh
  lemon juice
— 15 ml ($^1/_2$ oz) sugar syrup
— 60 ml (2 oz) Prosecco
— 1 scoop of homemade
  lemon sorbet (page 209)
— 1 scoop of crushed ice
  (roughly 150g/5 oz)
— 1 lemon, for zest garnish

Elegante

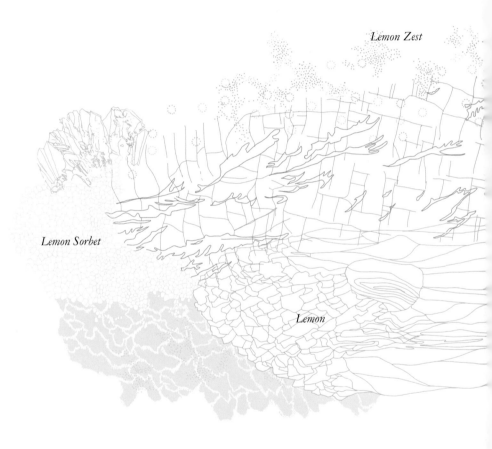

Lemon Zest

Lemon Sorbet

Lemon

FIGURE 1: Elegante—Flavor and Aroma Journey

Prosecco

Sweet Manhattan

1. Combine all the ingredients except the cherry in a cocktail tin over cubed ice.

2. Stir and then strain into a small, chilled coupette. Garnish with a Marasca cherry.

INGREDIENTS
— 40 ml (1^1/$_3$ oz) bourbon
— 20 ml (^{2}/$_3$ oz) sweet vermouth
— 2.5 ml (^{1}/$_2$ tsp) maraschino
— 3 dashes of Angostura bitters
— Marasca cherry, to garnish

Vintage Manhattan ^{2004}

It was after receiving a gift of 1920s Dubonnet that I first became interested in the play between what is "classic" and what is "vintage." I was amazed how good it tasted—the residual air in the bottle had both matured and mellowed the flavors. I was struck by the thought that the evolution of drinks is almost Darwinian: the best ones outlast their competition, and many have survived from before the turn of the twentieth century. Following the theory of evolution, I then wondered if it was possible to make the best ones even better without just changing the obvious components of product and proportion.

The powerful flavors of the Manhattan made this an ideal candidate for my first experimentation. After reading a number of papers, I was particularly inspired by a piece by Harold McGee in which he talked about the effect of oxidation on wine. I wondered if I could use oxidation in a positive way, controlling the process and thus refortifying not only the sweet vermouth but also the bourbon.

I started the process using a test batch of different bourbons and vermouths with varying proportions of alcohol, sealing staves inside the bottles, and storing them in cupboards. I mixed the Manhattan in a large bowl and poured it into old bourbon bottles, which were sterilized and dried, making sure that I left an air gap of 2.5 cm (1 inch) from the top of

VINTAGE MANHATTAN MIX
— 450 ml (15 oz) rye whisky
— 225 ml (7^1/$_2$ oz) sweet vermouth
— 200 microliters Angostura bitters

SINGLE SERVING
— 50 ml (1^3/$_4$ oz) Vintage Manhattan mix
— 2.5 ml (^{1}/$_2$ tsp) maraschino
— Marasca cherry, to garnish

the cap and taping the bottle with electrical tape to control oxidation. I had to ensure a consistent temperature all year round and so left them in a cellar where the sunlight would not be able to penetrate. I tested each bottle after six months, but the flavor didn't quite strike the nerve I was after. I left the bottles for a further five months and the flavors they released when tasted were complex, punchy, and yet soft—an incredible combination. In a freshly made Manhattan there is a distinct line where the vermouth begins and the bourbon ends—I find that I can even time this line when drinking. Very much like a young wine, it has fresh, pleasant characteristics. With the aged Manhattan this line dissipates, the flavors collapse in on themselves, and the drink becomes unpredictable, with a lengthy flavor that reverberates until the last sip.

Continuing with trial and error of different bourbons, vermouths, and aging times, I made 48 bottles of Manhattan 2:1 (the ratio of 13-year-old rye whisky to sweet vermouth), with 0.29 of Angostura bitters. I found that the higher the ABV (alcohol by volume) of the rye whisky, the better the process worked, to the point where even after just six months of aging, the Manhattan had a delicious taste. I have opened bottles from this batch each year since 2004. The longer each bottle spends aging, the more its flavors peak and spike as the chemicals of the alcohol react with one another. From one year onward, all the flavors of the Manhattan are accentuated and fill the mouth; the vermouth feels richer, the bourbon heavier. It makes for an elegant and decadent cocktail with a powerful aroma, which lingers on the glass for hours afterward. The six-year vintage has an incredibly long finish, enormous body, and a gentle hue like a vintage tawny port. Its flavors truly weigh on the tongue—it's a Manhattan with the volume turned all the way up!

1. To make the Vintage Manhattan mix, combine the rye whisky, sweet vermouth, and bitters and pour into a 750 ml bottle, leaving 2.5 cm (1 inch) at the top.

2. Tightly seal with a cap and waterproof tape. Leave for a minimum of 6 months in a cool, dark place.

For a single serving:

1. Combine the Vintage Manhattan mix and maraschino in a cocktail tin and stir over cubed ice.

2. Strain and pour into a small, chilled coupette. Garnish with a Marasca cherry.

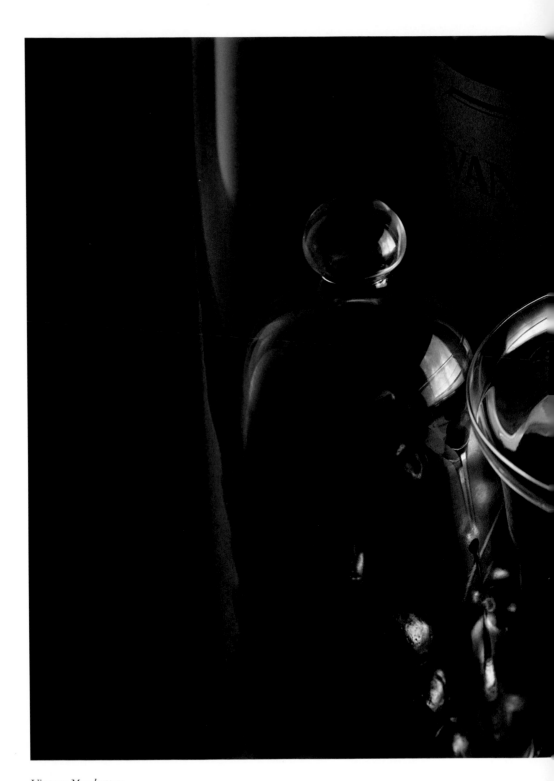

Vintage Manhattan

Sazerac

1. Combine all the ingredients except the absinthe over cubed ice in a cocktail tin.

2. Shake and fine strain into an absinthe-rinsed rocks glass.

INGREDIENTS
— 50 ml (1^2/$_3$ oz)
  Rittenhouse Rye
— 10 ml (2 tsp) sugar syrup
— 3 dashes of Peychaud's
  bitters
— 15 ml (^{1}/$_2$ oz) absinthe,
  to rinse glass

The Wink ^{2003}

One of the most alluring aspects of the drinking experience is that a bar is an accepted environment in which to indulge in cheeky repartee. The interaction between customer and bartender is extremely important, and it inspired this coyly named drink.

While working at the extremely busy Lonsdale House, visiting friends often complained to me that they couldn't get a drink fast enough. A remedy to this malady was found in the form of a surreptitious wink, whereby friends would walk in and wink at me to indicate the number of drinks they desired. As they were avid gin drinkers at the time (and still are, I'm sure), the wink denoted a form of gin Sazerac. The Peychaud's Bitters and gin complement the orange note that pops up in the middle of the drink, and the absinthe rinse on the glass induces a delicious aroma and subtle taste.

When this cocktail later found its way onto menus, it became the waiter or waitress who delivered the wink to the customer as they set the drink down.

1. Combine the gin, triple sec, syrup, and bitters over cubed ice in a cocktail tin.

2. Shake and fine-strain into a small absinthe-rinsed rocks glass. To finish, spritz the orange zest over the drink and discard.

INGREDIENTS
— 40 ml (1^2/$_3$ oz) gin
— 10 ml (2 tsp) triple sec
— 15 ml (^{1}/$_2$ oz) sugar syrup
— 2 dashes of Peychaud's
  bitters
— 15 ml (^{1}/$_2$ oz) absinthe,
  to rinse glass
— Orange twist (page 221),
  to finish

The Wink

Oh Gosh

Daiquiri

1. Combine all the ingredients except the lime wedge over cubed ice in a cocktail tin.

2. Shake hard and double strain into a large, chilled coupette. Garnish with a lime wedge on the rim.

— 50 ml (1^2/$_3$ oz) 3-year-old rum
— 20 ml (^{2}/$_3$ oz) fresh lime juice
— 10 ml (2 tsp) sugar syrup
— Lime wedge, to garnish

Oh Gosh ^{2000}

There are moments in bartending that are "sink or swim" for the bartender, none more so than when a regular customer asks, "Can you make me something slightly different today?" At Dick's Bar at The Atlantic I had a quintessentially English regular, a brain surgeon by profession, who drank nothing but daiquiris—mostly in large quantities. Having been put on the spot by his unusual request, rather than relying on a repertoire of back-up rum drinks, I decided to take out one shot of rum from the usual daiquiri and replace it with triple sec, garnishing with a lemon twist.

This simple movement resulted in a daiquiri with three levels of citrus: deep orange, tangy lime, and a light, zesty, lemon finish. Just after his first sip, the brain surgeon wobbled on his stool and remarked, "Oh Gosh!" Thus it was christened.

1. Combine all the ingredients except the lemon twist over cubed ice in a cocktail tin.

2. Shake hard and double strain into a large, chilled coupette. Finish with a lemon twist.

INGREDIENTS
— 25 ml (^{3}/$_4$ oz) 3-year-old rum
— 25 ml (^{3}/$_4$ oz) triple sec
— 15 ml (^{1}/$_2$ oz) fresh lime juice
— 10 ml (2 tsp) sugar syrup
— Lemon twist (page 221), to finish

Dry Ice Daiquiri ²⁰¹⁰

Makes 2

The Cocktail Lab | 34 — Tony Conigliaro

While in Cuba, I became engaged in a discussion, lamenting in tone, on how blended daiquiris melt so quickly in the sweltering Cuban climate. I love the texture of a properly blended drink, and a truly delicious cocktail will retain both its texture and temperature right until you (sadly) reach the bottom of the glass.

A while before this discussion took place, I had been experimenting with a dry-ice ice cream in classic cocktail flavors. Dry ice freezes the ice cream faster and with smaller crystals, which makes for a smoother ice cream. I couldn't see why the same technique shouldn't work for a daiquiri.

The temperature of the drink is set at 6°C (21°F), and it stays this cold for the duration of its consumption. A pleasing side effect of this is that the lime takes on a sherbet-like fizz. While being blended, the gas from the dry ice evaporates, which is incredibly theatrical to watch. Once all the gas has dissipated you know that the drink is ready. A few bubbles are left in order to retain a subtle fizzing quality. The ultimate blended daiquiri!

1. Combine all the liquid ingredients in a blender.

2. With the motor running, very slowly and carefully add the dry ice through the hole in the lid (always wear protective gloves when handling dry ice). Pour into a coupette to serve.

INGREDIENTS
— 100 ml (3^1/$_2$ oz) Havana Blanco
— 50 ml (1^3/$_4$ oz) fresh lime juice
— 60 ml (2 oz) gomme syrup
— 240 ml (1 cup) mineral water
— 100 g (3^1/$_2$ oz) dry ice

Flintlock ²⁰¹¹

The Flintlock is a complex combination of antique-feeling ingredients. Gunpowder tea was very popular at the turn of the 20th century and, for a green tea, has an incredibly bold flavor. It works in this drink by harmonizing with the green tea, while the Dandelion & Burdock bitters adds a touch of anise, mirroring the licorice present in the gin. Fernet Branca rounds off these flavors with its subtle, herbaceous flavor lingering upon the glass.

The name references the type of gun used at the turn of the century that used flint to ignite gunpowder; the resulting smell of the smoke once the gunpowder is lit also contributes to the drink in both an olfactory and sensory fashion. When serving the drink at the bar, we accompany this with a ball of flash cotton (see page 219), set alight at the table as a theatrical extra. When lit, it flames very quickly and then disappears.

1. Add cubed ice to a small rocks glass, along with the Fernet Branca. In a cocktail tin, combine the gin, Gunpowder tincture, and bitters, and stir.

2. Discard the Fernet Branca and ice, and strain the drink into the rocks glass. Serve with the ball of flash cotton, set alight alongside the drink.

INGREDIENTS
— 15 ml ($^1/_2$ oz) Fernet Branca, to rinse glass
— 50 ml ($1^2/_3$ oz) London Dry gin
— 15 ml ($^1/_2$ oz) gunpowder tincture (page 188)
— 3 dashes of Dr. Adam Elmegirab's Dandelion & Burdock bitters
— Ball of flash cotton (page 219), to serve

Egg Nog

1. Beat the egg yolks with the sugar to form a batter. Add the cream and milk and whisk thoroughly. Continue whisking while adding the bourbon and spiced rum slowly.

2. In a separate bowl, whisk the egg whites until they form stiff peaks, then fold the whites into the batter mix.

3. Serve in a large bowl and ladle into small cups. Sprinkle with grated nutmeg.

INGREDIENTS
— 6 eggs, separated
— 300 g (1^{1}/$_{4}$ cups) sugar
— 600 ml (2^{1}/$_{2}$ cups) light whipping cream
— 1.1 liters (4^{1}/$_{2}$ cups) whole milk
— 180 ml (^{3}/$_{4}$ cup) bourbon
— 180 ml (^{3}/$_{4}$ cup) spiced rum
— 1 tbsp freshly grated nutmeg, to finish

Somerset Egg Nog ²⁰¹⁰

As with food, drink recipes (particularly punch) are passed down via families and friends, with each generation adding its own twists. I first sampled, and then inherited, this recipe from Dale DeGroff, who in turn was taught it by his uncle Angelo. Dale's recipe uses bourbon and spiced rum and I exchanged these for cider brandy and cider.

Cider brandy gives this drink a wonderful kick while simultaneously adding spice and dryness. The carbonation of the cider makes the mix fluffy. On paper the ingredients suggest a heavy, stocky drink, but the order and method ensure that the end product is light and yielding.

1. Beat the egg yolks with the sugar to form a batter. Add the cream and milk and whisk thoroughly. Continue whisking while slowly adding the cider and cider brandy.

2. In a separate bowl, whisk the egg whites until they form stiff peaks. Fold the whites into the batter mix.

3. Serve in a large bowl and ladle into small cups or glasses.

4. To garnish, grate fresh apple over the drink and top each cup with a sprinkling of grated nutmeg.

INGREDIENTS
— 6 eggs, separated
— 300 g (1^{1}/$_{4}$ cups) sugar
— 300 ml (1^{1}/$_{4}$ cups) light whipping cream
— 600 ml (2^{1}/$_{2}$ cups) whole milk
— 150 ml (5 oz) Breton cider
— 150 ml (5 oz) 5-year Somerset cider brandy
— Freshly grated apple and nutmeg, to garnish

Somerset Egg Nog

El Presidente

El Presidente

1. Combine all the ingredients except the orange twist in a cocktail tin and stir over cubed ice.

2. Strain into a small, chilled coupette. Finish with an orange twist.

INGREDIENTS
— 40 ml (1$^1/_3$ oz) Havana Club Barrel Proof rum
— 20 ml ($^2/_3$ oz) sweet vermouth
— 10 ml (2 tsp) triple sec
— 5 ml (1 tsp) homemade grenadine (page 182)
— Orange twist (page 221), to garnish

Consulate ²⁰⁰⁹

The Cuban classic El Presidente is one of my all-time favorite drinks. The cocktail was named in honor of Cuban president Gerardo Machado, who ruled through most of the Prohibition years. Suitably distinguished in nature, this version is a lighter, more summery version of the El Presidente. The peach and sherry notes match the golden rum, and the sherry gently coaxes out the sour facet present in sweet vermouth.

1. Combine all the ingredients except the orange twist in a cocktail tin and stir over cubed ice.

2. Strain into a small, chilled coupette. Finish with an orange twist.

INGREDIENTS
— 40 ml (1$^1/_3$ oz) golden rum
— 20 ml ($^2/_3$ oz) sweet vermouth
— 10 ml (2 tsp) fino sherry
— 5 ml (1 tsp) crème de pêche
— Orange twist (page 221), to garnish

Ramos Gin Fizz

1. Combine all the ingredients in a cocktail shaker with a splash of sparkling water.

2. Shake vigorously over cubed ice until there is no ice whatsoever left in the shaker.

3. Strain into a highball glass and top with sparkling water.

INGREDIENTS
— 45 ml ($1^1/_2$ oz) gin
— 25 ml ($^3/_4$ oz) light whipping cream
— 25 ml ($^3/_4$ oz) egg white
— 25 ml ($^3/_4$ oz) sugar syrup
— 15 ml ($^1/_2$ oz) fresh lemon juice
— 15 ml ($^1/_2$ oz) fresh lime juice
— 5 ml (1 tsp) maraschino
— 2 dashes of orange blossom water
— Sparkling water, preferably Vichy Catalan, to top

Almond Ramos [2007]

Makes 2

Ferran Adrià's foray into foams demonstrates how to crown a drink with a frothy foam that endures until the very last sip. I wanted to use this technology to replicate the texture of a classic Ramos but with a lighter feel.

To do this, I replaced the dairy element of the original recipe with *latte di mandorla*—the Italian almond milk I used to drink as a child. This is great for those who prefer their drinks without dairy. The pairing of almond and maraschino cherry is a classic combination in the pastry world, and it works equally well here in liquid form.

The foam, produced by a siphon, traps flavor, both aerating and accentuating it for an incredibly light drink without any compromising punch. Fans of the Almond Ramos say it tastes like a cloud. (They may have had one too many...) Note that these ingredients are measured by weight, not volume.

1. Add all the ingredients to an ISI siphon charged with an N_2O gas charger.

2. Chill in the fridge for 30 minutes or until cooled.

3. Release the foam by pressing the lever and pour into a Ramos glass.

INGREDIENTS
— 60 g (2 oz) Beefeater gin
— 25 g (1 oz) egg white
— 15 g ($^1/_2$ oz) lemon juice
— 15 g ($^1/_2$ oz) lime juice
— 10 g ($^1/_3$ oz) sugar syrup
— 5 g maraschino
— 0.5 g orange blossom water
— 212 g ($7^1/_2$ oz) almond milk (page 171)
— 1 N_2O gas charger

Almond Ramos

Rhubarb Royale

Kir Royale

1. Build in a champagne flute and gently stir to mix.

INGREDIENTS
— 15 ml ($^1/_2$ oz) cassis
— 115 ml (4 oz) champagne

Rhubarb Royale

Ordering a Royale before dinner in France will present you with an abundance of tantalizing options. Rather than limiting themselves to using only cassis, the French offer such liqueurs as crème de mûre, poire, or framboise as a delicious addition to a glass of champagne.

I took this as inspiration for a more British take on the Kir Royale. I combined a homemade British rhubarb cordial with rhubarb liqueur, finishing off with Nyetimber—a fantastic English sparkling wine. Rhubarb and sparkling wine are a great marriage: the beautiful rose color gives way to the dryness of the wine, allowing the slight tartness of the rhubarb to really shine through. The result is a minimal and delicious aperitif—a perfect start to the evening.

1. Build in a 150 ml (5 oz) champagne flute and gently stir to mix.

INGREDIENTS
— 15 ml ($^1/_2$ oz) rhubarb
cordial (page 168)
— 15 ml ($^1/_2$ oz) rhubarb
liqueur (page 182)
— 115 ml (4 oz) sparkling
wine or champagne

New York Sour

1. Combine the bourbon, lemon juice, egg white, and sugar syrup in a cocktail tin.

2. Dry shake, then shake over cubed ice. Strain and pour into a large, chilled coupette.

3. Pour in the claret last (this avoids aerating and diluting the flavor of the wine through shaking).

INGREDIENTS
— 50 ml (1¹/₂ oz) bourbon
— 25 ml (³/₄ oz) fresh lemon juice
— 25 ml (³/₄ oz) egg white
— 15 ml (¹/₂ oz) sugar syrup
— 10 ml (2 tsp) claret

Spitfire [2010]

I have always enjoyed a New York or Boston Sour— bourbon sours with a claret or port float—but neither was a drink that I particularly felt like having in the summer. I was after a lighter version for balmy evenings and began by matching a cognac sour with a peach liqueur that would draw out the fruity element present in cognac. In turn, I wanted to dry out and lengthen the flavor of peach while ensuring it wasn't too sweet. I added white wine, purposely choosing an Ugni Blanc, which is made from the same grape as cognac and mirrors its slight peachy notes.

The 69 Colebrooke Row house cognac was formulated with the Spitfire in mind. Gilles and son Luc of the Merlet family are long-term associates of mine. I went to them to create a cognac that was drinkable in itself but with a bounty of fruity notes that would sit underneath the peach flavor. In response, they sent me eight samples with tasting notes. I tasted each of these on their own, made a range of classic cocktails, and finally used them in a Spitfire.

The Spitfire changed the way I think about the structure of cocktails. At first glance this drink seems to combine ingredients that don't appear to work together. However, the framework of a cocktail recipe has a formula just like a sheet of music. You can take this formula and play it in one key, but it will also work if you play it in a higher or lower key. It was with this in mind that I was able to achieve an incredible harmony of flavors where the peach acts as a bridge between all the ingredients.

INGREDIENTS
— 40 ml (1¹/₃ oz) cognac
— 25 ml (³/₄ oz) fresh lemon juice
— 25 ml (³/₄ oz) egg white
— 15 ml (¹/₂ oz) sugar syrup
— 10 ml (2 tsp) crème de pêche
— 25 ml (³/₄ oz) dry white wine

1. Combine the cognac, lemon juice, egg white, sugar syrup, and crème de pêche in a cocktail tin.

2. Dry shake and then shake over cubed ice. Strain into a large, chilled coupette and pour in the dry white wine last (this avoids aerating and diluting the flavor of the wine through shaking).

Spitfire

2.
CULINARY
SKILLS

Culinary Skills

For a long time there has been a blatant divide between the two crafts of food and drink. The last few years have witnessed the record development of a more open exchange between chefs and bartenders in a way that was previously only experienced by sommeliers. The psychology and physiology of the two professions are of course different, but they have an undeniable overlap. Both consider sensitivity of the mouth and the way that flavor works, and both forever seek new ingredients, methods, and processes to release, revive, and reinforce flavor.

Over the years I have developed a long-standing relationship with the chef Bruno Loubet, which began in 1998 while we were working at the restaurant and bar Isola. This meeting of minds marked the beginning of my first bout of real creative freedom. It was during this time that I developed an interest in watching pastry chefs and the way they manipulated ingredients, particularly in the making of purées and utilizing the flavor profiles of fruit and vegetables. I ceased simply looking through the lens of a bartender, broadening the spectrum of ingredients that I worked with.

At this time, seasonality was a new way of thinking and a novel enterprise. I began to visit farmers' markets and build relationships with individual farmers; this ensured that the fruit I was using had never been frozen and had no traveling time. The farmers would call me with news of seasonal stock and then I'd buy directly from them. This was a unique idea for cocktail making. Since then, a new era has dawned in which chefs are now paying attention to drinks more than ever before, and now cocktails have even arrived in three-Michelin-star restaurants. Chefs have led the way in the past, but our project as bartenders is different; for a long time it has been my aim to branch out from where they began.

Although I continue to employ chefs' techniques and utilize the skills of the culinary world, I reached a certain point where I realized that the focus should be on creating our own bartending language. The time that a drink actually spends in your mouth is much shorter than the longevity of a chewed ingredient, and there is less repeated retronasal experience; therefore the opportunity a bartender has to execute flavor is very narrow. The fact that texture is also minimal means that we are relying almost entirely on a perception of flavor—it's like we are taking the sense of touch out of flavor, or separating the sense of touch.

The following drink recipes trace the progress made from the very beginning of my relationship with chefs and fruit suppliers, going on to explore a new awareness in working with seasonality and translating this to function practically within the bar world.

Chefs have led the way in the past, but our project as bartenders is different; for a long time it has been my aim to branch out from where they began.

Sweet Broiled Lemon Margarita

This simple twist on a classic margarita is the brainchild of my first foray into observing the cooking techniques of chefs. Broiling the lemon relieves the fruit of its acid bite by caramelizing the fructose and killing its vitamin C.

The flavor of the lemon after juicing takes on a delicious, deep, sultry caramel note that makes it a perfect match for the caramel and toffee notes found in a reposado tequila. I like to use a dry triple sec, such as Merlet, to balance the sweetness of the broiled lemon with a dry finish. This version of the margarita has an incredibly smooth and soft finish, making it hard to have only one!

1. Combine all the ingredients except the sugar in a cocktail tin and shake over cubed ice.

2. Fine strain and pour into a chilled coupette with a half sugar rim.

INGREDIENTS
— 50 ml (1 1/2 oz) reposado tequila
— 25 ml (3/4 oz) broiled lemon juice (page 164)
— 20 ml (2/3 oz) triple sec
— Sugar, for the rim

Sweet Broiled Lemon Margarita

Apple Mojito

Apple Mojito ¹⁹⁹⁹

Serving cocktails every day, rather than consuming them, can leave a bartender hankering for more than just water for refreshment. I began playing around with fruit juices, hoping for something more flavorful and invigorating. I found that a great way of achieving this is simply to exchange the rum in a mojito with freshly pressed apple juice.

There are heaps of detox properties in every element of this drink. As a whole, the three major components are fantastic for facilitating and improving digestion. In addition, lime juice works hard to rejuvenate the skin, apples aid in preventing anemia and weakness, and mint helps with both headaches and nausea and activates the saliva glands to promote taste.

For those not drinking alcohol, habitually or exceptionally, there's no reason not to be drinking something really good. This is simple to make, especially in batches. Of course, when good intentions fail, simply substitute the apple juice for a delicious dark rum!

1. Muddle the mint sprigs with the sugar syrup in a cocktail tin.

2. Mix in the lemon and lime juices, then add crushed ice and the apple juice.

3. Shake twice and then pour the mixture into a highball glass.

4. Garnish with a lemon and lime slice and a bruised mint sprig.

INGREDIENTS
— 6 mint sprigs
— 15 ml (½ oz) sugar syrup
— 10 ml (2 tsp) fresh lemon juice
— 15 ml (½ oz) fresh lime juice
— 75 ml (2½ oz) freshly pressed green apple juice
— Lemon and lime slice and mint sprig, to garnish

Gooseberry and Elderflower Collins

Few drinks are as refreshing as the Tom Collins on a hot summer afternoon, and this version began life as a platform for the delicious—but unfortunately short-lived—gooseberry season, which lasts for just two to three weeks in August.

The gooseberry resonates with a sharp and sour tang, which is balanced by the acidity of the lemon and the deep, mellow flavor of the elderflower. Although I originally made this drink with gooseberry syrup, over time technology (and multiple trials and errors) led to the discovery that homemade cordials worked much better in many cocktails—this one included. The cordial has the same proportions as the syrup, combining sugar, water, and elderflower, but it has a much fresher and cleaner finish.

The first batch of gooseberry gin I made was 35 liters (9 gallons), and I thought this would last a long time. However, it sold extremely quickly and I had to wait an entire year to make the next batch!

1. In a highball glass, build the gooseberry gin, lemon juice, and elderflower cordial over cubed ice.

2. Gently stir with a bar spoon.

3. Finish with soda, and garnish with a lemon wedge and a gooseberry.

INGREDIENTS
— 50 ml (1 1/2 oz) gooseberry gin (page 210)
— 25 ml (3/4 oz) fresh lemon juice
— 20 ml (2/3 oz) homemade elderflower cordial (page 169)
— Soda water, to top
— Lemon wedge and single gooseberry, to garnish

Gooseberry and Elderflower Collins

Fig and Licorice Caipirinha

Fig and Licorice Caipirinha [2000]

Ploughing through the pastry books in the kitchen at Isola, I was occupied by a constant search for fresh flavor combinations. Rather than simply turning to classic cocktails and cocktail books, for the first time I began to research classical desserts for inspiration.

I uncovered an old pastry recipe that used fig and licorice and I began to translate this combination back to the bartending world. Although the lifespan of the fig is very short, it's well worth using fresh figs in this recipe; fig syrups or liqueurs never fully replicate the flavor of real fig. The flavor links between the cachaça, fig, and licorice are made in heaven.

1. Muddle all the ingredients in a cocktail tin and add crushed ice.

2. Shake briskly and pour into a rocks glass. Garnish with a fig slice.

INGREDIENTS
— 50 ml (1²/₃ oz) cachaça
— 1 lime, cut into 8 wedges
— 1 ripe fig, skinned and cut into 8 pieces
— 15 ml (¹/₂ oz) licorice syrup
— Fig slice, to garnish

Fruit Gin and Tonics ²⁰⁰⁵

Bitter Lemon, Grapefruit, Raspberry, Blood Orange

Working with fruit in cocktails pivots upon two factors: the quality of the fruit and the process by which you combine it with the alcohol. I was dissatisfied with the off note often produced by macerating fruit; I wanted a truly fresh flavor—a super-clean imprint of the fruit onto the alcohol. I observed the way in which pastry chefs cook fruit sous vide and could see no reason why this principle couldn't also be applied to cooking fruit with alcohol.

The sous vide method (page 148) is essentially cooking at a low, controlled, and constant temperature using a water bath. Cooking in this way transports the flavor from the fruit to the gin incredibly effectively. The gin is placed into vacuum bags with the fruit and sealed. I never add any sugar as this unbalances the tonic. The alcohol is infused at a low temperature, which ensures that the structure doesn't fall apart. Controlling the temperature is important. If the temperature exceeds 52°C (125°F), the heat pulls apart the structure of the alcohol. The closed system allows cooking to take place without oxygen; this way the volatiles don't evaporate and none of the flavor or moisture is lost.

Audrey Saunders, dear friend and queen of the New York cocktail scene, inspired me with her recipe for bitter lemon gin. I began my own version by infusing gin with lemon peel. It works wonderfully in a stark drink such as the gin and tonic because the flavor can take center stage. It's important to use a gin that will stand up for itself, otherwise the fruit will overpower its complexities. It was a lengthy process to find the right balance between fruit and gin quantities; each fruit has its own point at which the best flavor match with the gin is obtained—and each fruit balances in a different way with the tonic. Fruit fibers have to be fine strained, or else the gin will keep changing its flavor. This can be done in a Büchner funnel (page 154).

1. Build the gin and tonic water over cubed ice and garnish with the corresponding fruit.

INGREDIENTS
— 50 ml (1²/₃ oz) fruit gin (see pages 199–202)
— 150 ml (5 oz) tonic water
— Fruit, to garnish

(Clockwise from top left) Bitter Lemon, Grapefruit, Blood Orange, and Raspberry Gins

Sicilian Sour

Sicilian Sour [2006]

In 1998, my grandmother's recipe book was unearthed. Its discovery revealed an incredible series of recipes for homemade liqueurs such as limoncello, crème de cacao, and amaretto. The amaretto recipe leapt out at me, comprised as it was of entirely natural ingredients. I loved the idea of using my grandmother's recipe in a cocktail that would be an honor both to her and to my family's Sicilian history.

My abiding memories of being a child in Sicily, other than the freedom of running around in the sunshine, are of flavors and scents. To recapture summers past, I called upon almonds, apricots, and lemons—a tasty triangle of Italian ingredients native to Sicily. Apricot pits and almond kernels are very similar and amaretto can be made from both. Amaretto has a bitter, as well as a sweet, note that is often overlooked, and this is complemented by the Angostura bitters. Using ingredients that inspire a different and drier tonality to amaretto, the Sicilian Sour is a delicious twist on a well-known drink.

1. Add all ingredients except the bitters and lemon slice to a cocktail tin.

2. Dry shake, then shake over cubed ice. Strain into a large, chilled coupette.

3. Garnish with a dash of bitters and a lemon slice on the edge of the glass, if liked.

INGREDIENTS
— 35 ml (1¼ oz) homemade amaretto (page 181)
— 15 ml (½ oz) apricot liqueur
— 25 ml (¾ oz) fresh lemon juice
— 25 ml (¾ oz) egg white
— 5 ml (1 tsp) sugar syrup
— Dash of Angostura bitters
— Lemon slice, to garnish (optional)

Marshmallow Milkshake ²⁰⁰⁶

I love milkshakes that are soft, foamy, and light. I spent some time looking at a history of American flavors and tried to utilize them in the milkshake format. The homemade mallow syrup really brings out the true earthy, woody, and creamy flavor of mallow—so much more delicious than the synthetic options. Using a siphon makes the mixture lighter and softer than using a blender. The result is a super-subtle set of flavors with a comforting moreishness to them.

1. Put all the ingredients into an ISI siphon charged with an N₂O gas charger.

2. Release the milkshake by pressing down on the lever, pour into a vintage milk bottle, and serve with a straw.

INGREDIENTS
— 70 ml (2¹/₃ oz) mallow syrup (page 180)
— 200 ml (6³/₄ oz) light whipping cream
— 200 ml (6³/₄ oz) whole milk
— 1 N₂O gas charger

Marshmallow Milkshake

Bellini

Giuseppe Cipriani, the founder of the infamous Harry's Bar in Venice, created the Bellini around the time of the Second World War. His recipe was simply white peach purée topped with Prosecco. Cipriani named his drink in honor of the Venetian painter Giovanni Bellini because its peachy, fleshy hue matched the skin tones used in his work. He always stirred the Prosecco and the purée together, as I do here, which means you achieve an integrated drink with a rich foam.

Since its inception, the Bellini has enjoyed enduring popularity for the simple way it packs in flavor, and for being refreshing and glamorous in equal measure. Although wine can be a complex ingredient to work with, its low ABV broadens the space for flavor to really shine through, and the versatility of Prosecco also makes it ideal for fruits other than peach. It is important, however, to allow the integrity of the Prosecco to remain by pairing it with a fruit that can sit within the framework of the Prosecco without masking its flavors, such as the suggestions that follow.

Working in accordance with the seasons means that I am constantly discovering new combinations of flavors and updating my recipe book. Good-quality fresh fruit is vital, but you can freeze your purées if you want.

1. First pour the purée into a cocktail tin, then add the Prosecco.

2. Stir very gently so as not to burst the bubbles in the Prosecco. Strain into a champagne flute or tumbler.

INGREDIENTS
— 50 ml (1³/₄ oz) peach purée
— 100 ml (3¹/₂ oz) Prosecco

Fruit Bellini [2004]

Wild Strawberry & Neroli

This recipe began life as a foodie joke but soon became one of my favorite Bellini combinations. It was Hervé This who first showed me that the chemical difference between strawberries and wild strawberries can be imitated by adding lemon juice, orange blossom water, and sugar to regular strawberries.

To the "wild" strawberry purée I added a hint of neroli, an essential oil derived from orange blossom. The strawberry, neroli, and Prosecco all share a chemical overlap that creates an incredible flow of flavors. See the purée recipe on page 204.

Cherry Blossom & Almond

The acidity level of cherries can be hard to regulate, making a good purée difficult to achieve. To remedy this, once the purée is made I check the acidity with a Brix meter (see page 160) and a pH level meter. The resulting Bellini is fruity, tart, and juicy, with a subtle hint of marzipan. See the purée recipe on page 205.

Pear & Green Tea

I love the flavor of Bartlett pears, which have a fantastic juiciness and are a brilliant match for the flavors of Prosecco. It is important to use a very high-quality Japanese matcha powder. This slight Japanese twist on the Bellini, first made at the restaurant Roka, has a delicious juicy/dry dichotomy alongside a slightly tannic finish. See the purée recipe on page 205.

Pumpkin

Using this vegetable in a cocktail sounds a little off-key, but the pumpkin purée is an incredible match for Prosecco, with a vivid orange hue. See the purée recipe on page 204.

1. First pour the purée into a cocktail tin, then add the Prosecco.

2. Stir very gently so as not to burst the bubbles in the Prosecco. Strain into a champagne flute or tumbler.

INGREDIENTS
— 50 ml ($1^3/_4$ oz) fruit purée (see opposite and pages 204–5)
— 100 ml ($3^1/_2$ oz) Prosecco

Pictured on following pages

Fruit Bellinis

Nettle Gimlet ²⁰¹⁰

Britain has a long history of earthy, simple, tasty cuisine. The national flavor psyche of beet, nettle, cabbage, dandelion, and sorrel has recently experienced a justly deserved revival in popularity. I tentatively ordered nettle, leek, and goat's curd soup at a restaurant in Soho recently, unsure of what to expect but anticipating the worst! The only experience I'd really had with nettles was falling into a giant bed of them when I was young. Putting this to one side, I dived in and it was fantastic—not at all what I had expected!

I took advantage of this renaissance of British flavor and created a twist on the classic Gimlet using traditional dried nettles. I looked at nettle cordial recipes that dated back to the 1800s and realized how simply they could be made. I tried recipes with both fresh and dried nettles, but the dried produced a range of beautiful tannic notes. I use a dehydrator to dry the leaves, but you could just as easily turn the nettles upside down and dry them by a window.

The resulting cordial is surprisingly fruity and reminiscent of elderflowers. The grassy flavor of nettles works well with the orris root, angelica, and juniper botanicals in gin. The subtleties of the spirit are left undiminished and are complemented rather than softened by the fruitiness of the cordial.

The Nettle Gimlet is quirky yet grown-up—a conceptual but very drinkable reimagining of the Gimlet proper.

1. Combine the gin and cordial in a cocktail tin and stir over cubed ice.

2. Strain into a small, chilled coupette and finish with a small lemon twist.

INGREDIENTS
— 40 ml (1¹/₃ oz) gin
— 20 ml (²/₃ oz) nettle cordial (page 169)
— Lemon twist (page 221), to finish

Nettle Gimlet

Rhubarb Gimlet ²⁰¹¹

The natural progression of my interest in the Gimlet remained British in nature and continued to work in accordance with the seasons. I love rhubarb for its complex set of flavors that loans itself to a broad spectrum of cocktails, and in particular rhubarb and gin are a perfect match. The Rhubarb Gimlet is a cocktail with a neat circle of flavors; simple, pared down, and minimal, with a seasonal twist.

1. Combine the gin and cordial in a cocktail tin and stir over cubed ice.

2. Strain into a small, chilled coupette.

3. Finish with a grapefruit twist.

INGREDIENTS
— 40 ml (1^1/$_3$ oz) gin
— 20 ml (^{2}/$_3$ oz) homemade rhubarb cordial (page 168)
— Grapefruit twist, to finish (page 221)

Somerset Sour ²⁰⁰⁹

Creating a cocktail that can be enjoyed during a specific season is a real driving force behind many of my recipes. If the Spitfire is a more summery version of a New York Sour, then the Somerset Sour does the same for autumn. For me, autumn is epitomized by the flavors and aromas associated with Halloween: the smell of hay, toffee, and bobbing apples. I wanted to encapsulate these in a drink and in doing so orchestrate a shared nostalgia of autumn for every drinker.

Cider brandy is distilled at autumn time, and although it was an ingredient that I had never worked with before, I chose it as the base of this cocktail because it really captures the taste of apples at this time of year. The layering of ingredients was as important to this Sour as in the Spitfire; adding cognac dries out the cider brandy while introducing an element of toffee-like richness; the cider float ensures a crisp and refreshing finish. I discovered that the food-grade essence cIS-3-Hexenal had the perfect "just-cut grass" note that, when added to fresh apple, makes it taste and smell just like hay.

During the process of putting together this drink, I was always aware that an apple slice would be a complementary garnish. However, when experimenting with how to stop the apple from browning, it occurred to me that the scoops of apples I was testing would look just like bobbing apples if they were floating in the foam on the Sour. I began by using a melon baller to scoop a variety of apples until I discovered one with the best absorbing qualities—the Pink Lady. If the cIS-3-Hexenal is added with pectin and sorbic acid then the apple is prevented from browning. The resulting apples are incredibly juicy but also crisp from the pectin and acid, with a faint aroma of hay. The mini bobbing apples float in the foam of the Sour to create a garnish that both parallels the flavors of the drink and enhances them with a multidimensional and multisensory flavor experience. This really expands upon the idea of what a garnish can be.

INGREDIENTS
— 40 ml (1$^{1}/_{3}$ oz) cider brandy
— 10 ml (2 tsp) cognac
— 25 ml ($^{3}/_{4}$ oz) fresh lemon juice
— 25 ml ($^{3}/_{4}$ oz) hay-infused egg white (see page 73)
— 15 ml ($^{1}/_{2}$ oz) sugar syrup
— Dash of cider
— Bobbing apple (page 211), to garnish

Continues on page 73

Somerset Sour

Somerset Sour, continued

Aroma was a motivating factor behind this drink. Audrey Saunders and I have often lamented the unfortunate wet-dog-nose smell that arises from egg white reacting with alcohol. Together we have engaged in many conversations about how to eliminate it for good. I had a eureka moment when making truffle omelettes at home. I realized that the truffle flavored the eggs through scent. Quite simply, since eggs are porous they can absorb smells, and with this as the case, I could use any number of smells to flavor them. All that was needed was to create a controlled environment in which to flavor the eggs through aroma.

I conducted tests by soaking different food-grade hydrosols in cotton and sealing them in Tupperware with the eggs, keeping the box in the fridge. The aroma in the box then fills all the empty space, including seeping through the eggshell, which is semipermeable, meaning it will absorb small molecules around it and add flavor to the egg itself. With this knowledge I added to the egg white the same hay essence as I had injected into the bobbing apple.

1. Combine all the ingredients except the cider and bobbing apple in a cocktail tin.

2. Dry shake then shake over cubed ice. Strain and serve in a large, chilled coupette, floating the cider on top.

3. Garnish with hay-infused bobbing apple.

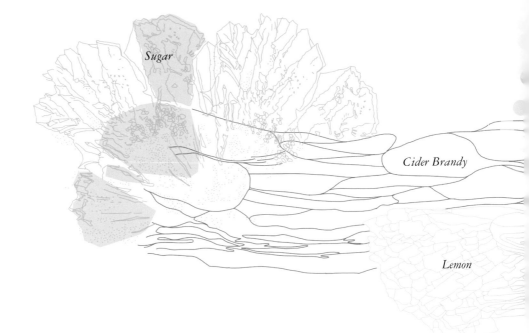

FIGURE 2: Somerset Sour—Flavor and Aroma Journey

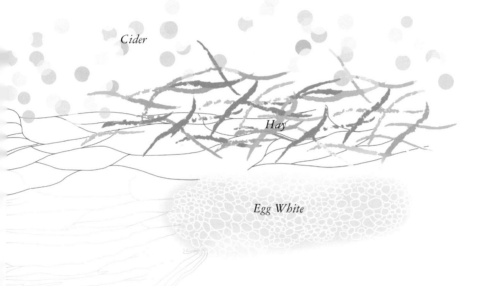

Cider

Hay

Egg White

Lime Plus + ²⁰¹⁰

This drink began life as a technical project to examine how lime flavor works. Lime is an integral ingredient in a multitude of cocktail recipes, yet in this country achieving consistency of flavor is often problematic as citrus fruits have to be imported from different parts of the globe. This means that the fruit has variants of sweetness and pH levels, and this can affect the consistency of a cocktail over time.

Enabling a uniformity of lime flavor while retaining a natural finish to the drink was no simple task, but the final result was one of extraordinary impact. I achieved a deep and multilayered lime flavor with a food-grade lime essential oil. This is married with homogenized lime juice for maximum flavor.

I added the lime essence directly to the cachaça in minute amounts using a micropipette, which allowed the lime flavor to really sing through the spirit. Waves and layers of lime reveal themselves in new forms as the drink is consumed.

1. To make the infused cachaça, add the lime essence to a bottle of cachaça.

For a single serving:

1. Combine the infused cachaça, fresh lime juice, egg white, and sugar syrup in a cocktail tin. Dry shake, then shake over cubed ice.

2. Strain into a large, chilled whisky glass, twist the lime zest over, and discard.

LIME-INFUSED CACHAÇA
— 750 ml (25$^1/_2$ oz) Leblon cachaça
— 750 microliters lime essence (page 191)

SINGLE SERVING
— 50 ml (1$^2/_3$ oz) lime-infused cachaça
— 30 ml (1 oz) fresh lime juice
— 25 ml ($^3/_4$ oz) egg white
— 15 ml ($^1/_2$ oz) sugar syrup
— Lime twist (page 221), to finish

Lime Plus +

3.
SAVORY

Savory

Modern drinking culture has substantiated the consumer's tendency to drink things that are sweet, especially during the latter part of the twentieth century. Drinking has long been associated with partying and therefore with sugar—nature's rocket fuel. The last decade has given birth to a growing interest in and understanding about flavor—both at the consumer and trade levels. I've witnessed a massive increase in the consumption of more savory drinks like the Negroni and Martini, and that is entirely down to customers understanding more about the way that they drink and challenging their own preconceptions. You don't need to have disco drinks to have fun!

This has perhaps helped the cocktail world to experience a recent savory revolution, reaching for botanicals and flavors that have been criminally overlooked for a long time. Appealing to the savory palate calls for a total overhaul of the ingredients most often employed, and especially for a reassessment of sugar content. For a bartender, the parameters of working with a savory drinks are therefore both interesting and challenging.

My interest in savory cocktails was first awakened by working in a number of bars that were linked to high-profile restaurants, and although this was never intentional, it's a circumstance I have always embraced. It has allowed me to see how cocktails work in a different context and with a different clientele. In restaurants, accuracy reaches new heights of importance; it is not just necessary for the drink to have balance within itself, but also with the food that is being consumed.

Food works on a different level and flavor boundaries change accordingly. I have always had a problem with specific cocktail and food pairing, as more often than not it ends up being a case of trying to force cocktails on food, and vice versa. Whenever I have designed drinks for restaurant menus I make sure that I take the food menu into account, but I have rarely designed cocktails with specific dishes in mind. While the spirituous end of cocktails can be far too strong to continue drinking through a meal, the sourness or sweetness of drinks can rip through the more delicate nuances of food. Therefore, I have always made sure that the cocktails I create are in smaller portions—no one can drink several normal-sized cocktails throughout the course of a meal, even if they really practice! Rather, I like to provide snippets of drinks that can enhance a menu, always taking into consideration how the chefs have thought out the food menu.

Doing this is usually a very long process that requires constantly tasting and retasting, but this practice has led to the creation of some of my favorite drinks. The following cocktails are drinks that either have been designed to be consumed with food or were inspired by using savory ingredients in a new way.

Appealing to the savory palate calls for a total overhaul of the ingredients most often employed.

White Truffle Martini ¹⁹⁹⁹

The White Truffle Martini was the first drink I ever created with the sole purpose of working within a savory stricture. With the Bloody Mary the reigning go-to of savory drinks, I wanted to open up the parameters of flavor combinations without creating a drink that would only have a niche appeal.

The Martini is a dry drink and accordingly lends itself well to a savory spin. White truffles have a delicious, decadent flavor, and combining them with dry vermouth plays upon both ingredients' earthy qualities. I made a julienne of the truffles and added just 1 gram of this to a bottle of vermouth, letting it macerate for one month. The same method can be used with black truffles but requires twice the amount of truffle and leaving it in the bottle for three months. The bottle should be full, sealed both with tape and a cap to avoid oxidation as much as possible, and then left in the fridge.

The white truffle is a luxurious and sensual product; adding it to an already stylish and graceful drink created an accessible Martini with a new layered profile. Originally conceived while working in an Italian restaurant, the White Truffle Martini proved to be extremely popular, especially as an aperitif.

1. Combine your choice of gin or vodka with the vermouth in a cocktail tin and stir over cubed ice.

2. Strain into a small, chilled coupette and garnish with a truffle shaving.

Variation: Black Truffle Martini

Simply replace the white truffle vermouth with black truffle vermouth (page 197).

INGREDIENTS
— 50 ml (1²/₃ oz) gin or 60 ml (2 oz) vodka
— 15 ml (¹/₂ oz) white truffle vermouth (page 197)
— Truffle shaving, to garnish

Black Truffle Martini

Luna

Luna ²⁰⁰³

The Luna was invented in collaboration with the renowned drinks writer and vodka expert Ian Wisniewski. The idea was to create a new profile for the vodka Martini but with already-existing vodkas, resulting in our "own blend." We began by conducting numerous in-depth vodka tastings and subsequently matched two for an interesting yet cohesive blend that would also lend itself to the vermouth.

Siwucha is a raw vodka, meaning that it is an incompletely rectified mix of two grain spirits. The mixture is then seasoned in oak barrels and a scent of forest fruit is added. I particularly like how the earthiness of the Siwucha underpins the drink. It adds incredible complexity, with varying musky and residual fusel oil (potato oil) notes.

The Moskovskaya vodka brings fresh mint and anise notes to the equation, which are enhanced by the vermouth and then lengthened by the bitters. There is a profound progression of notes, executed in a very simple way that gives you far more to hold on to than with your average vodka Martini. Collaborations with experts in their field bring an interesting outside perspective, which can really refresh what we do as bartenders.

1. Combine all the ingredients except the lemon twist in a cocktail tin and stir over cubed ice.

2. Strain into a chilled coupette and finish with a lemon twist.

INGREDIENTS
— 40 ml (1⅓ oz) Moskovskaya vodka
— 20 ml (⅔ oz) Siwucha vodka
— 10 ml (2 tsp) dry vermouth
— 1 dash of Angostura bitters
— Lemon twist (page 221), to finish

Noshino ²⁰⁰⁴

The cocktail enthusiast David Embury has written that the key to a perfectly executed cocktail is that the base, and what happens around the base, is the direction that the drink should take. Embury believed that a great drink should whet rather than dull the appetite; it should be dry, with sufficient alcoholic flavor, yet smooth and pleasing to both the palate and the eye. While working at the Shochu Lounge, I wanted to create an aperitif designed specifically with Japanese cuisine in mind but keeping in line with Embury's requirements. Shochu and sake reside in the same flavor band and together provide the base of this cocktail; the customer has the option of two garnishes—samphire or cucumber—which send the drink in opposite directions, in the same way that an olive or a twist will to a Martini.

Azure sake is made with deep-sea water collected from a natural spring located at the bottom of the Pacific Ocean, and it has a subtle, salty quality to it. The samphire garnish not only aesthetically replicates the seaweed in Japanese cooking, but it also plays to its saltiness. The cucumber option is much lighter, with a refreshing finish. I wanted to emulate the cut of sashimi for a complementary aesthetic and so carefully observed the head of sashimi while at work at the Shochu Lounge. He taught me how to use a sashimi knife correctly: rather than using the wrist in an up-and-down motion, cutting sashimi requires a sweeping, pulling-back action. I spent days cutting cucumbers, looking for the same sharp and angular lines.

This drink has simple ingredients, simple inflections of flavor, and an elegant aesthetic. Minimal and incredibly drinkable!

1. Combine the shochu and sake in a cocktail tin and stir over cubed ice.

2. Strain and pour into a sake glass. Garnish with either a cucumber slice or a strand of samphire.

INGREDIENTS
— 50 ml (1$^{1}/_{2}$ oz) Kigo shochu
— 25 ml ($^{3}/_{4}$ oz) Azure sake
— Cucumber slice or samphire strand, to garnish

Noshino

The Dry Martini ²⁰⁰⁷

The modern Martini is synonymous with "dryness," which indicates a small amount of vermouth added to the base spirit. The popularity of this style derives from the way we taste and use our mouth when drinking. The alcohol, herbs, and botanicals in both vermouth and gin provide a slight dryish feeling in your mouth. The mouth reacts to this and produces saliva, and in turn the stimulation of the saliva glands prepares your stomach for the prospect of food, producing that hungry feeling.

I wanted to take this process further. It occurred to me that by seeking out ingredients that stimulate dryness, I could then add those ingredients to the drink to enhance the dry sensation. This way, I wouldn't just be playing around with the structure of the Martini. Rather, I was after an ingredient that had no flavor of its own, which could change the cocktail in a simultaneously subtle and dramatic way while remaining true to classical proportions.

I spent a lot of time researching exactly how the tongue works and how flavors work once in the mouth. In order to taste, saliva breaks down the components of ingredients. I discovered that tannins and polyphenols, which are normally found in red wine and tea, work to shrink the protein chains in saliva. Grapes have a high content of tannins and polyphenols, and by extracting these I could make a tincture that would directly enhance the dryness that is already present in the vermouth. I peeled, dried, and made a concentrate of the skins and added a small amount to a bottle of vermouth. I later discovered that the presence of tannins and polyphenols is higher in the grape seeds and changed the tincture accordingly.

By adding this flavorless "dry essence tincture" (page 186), I was able to imbue the Dry Martini with a profundity that gives such depth and length that the drink becomes an entirely different experience. Carefully balanced, the dry essence tincture is not offensively dry, but rather it intensifies flavor by creating a closed circuit of taste in the mouth—an incredible flavor loop that keeps going until you

"Dry" Dry Vermouth
— 750 ml (25 $^1/_2$ oz) dry vermouth
— 150 microliters dry essence tincture (page 186)

Single Serving
— 50 ml (1 $^2/_3$ oz) gin
— 15 ml ($^1/_2$ oz) "Dry" dry vermouth
— Green Sicilian olive, to garnish

reach the juicy green olive waiting for you in the bottom of the glass.

1. To make the "dry" dry vermouth, add the dry essence tincture to a bottle of dry vermouth.

For a single serving:

1. Combine the gin and "dry" dry vermouth in a cocktail tin and stir over cubed ice.

2. Strain and pour into a small, chilled coupette. Garnish with a green Sicilian olive.

The Dry Martini

Dirty Martini by the Sea

Dirty Martini by the Sea ²⁰⁰⁸

The Dirty Martini by the Sea was created for a dinner event at Pontus Frithiof, in Stockholm, which brought together chefs and sommeliers to pair a small drinks menu with a range of original dishes. This version of a Dirty Martini uses Japanese seaweed cooked sous vide with vodka (page 203) and was created to match a seaweed and oyster dish named the Rock Pool.

I took the same slivers of purple seaweed that were used in the dish and cooked them sous vide with vodka to develop a beautiful purple tint. Using vodka rather than gin really allows the seaweed and vermouth to shine through in this cocktail. A later version had an intense olive bread crisp as a garnish. With the help of a chef I baked some olive bread, froze the loaf, and then used a meat slicer to cut it into thin slices. Each slice was then put back into the oven to heat through. The drink is served in a sake glass and works as a fantastic palate cleanser.

1. Combine the vodka and vermouth in a cocktail tin and stir over cubed ice.

2. Strain and pour into a chilled, small coupette, adding the olive. If you like, serve with crisp olive bread at the side of the glass.

INGREDIENTS
— 50 ml (1²/₃ oz) seaweed vodka (page 203)
— 10 ml (2 tsp) vermouth
— 1 baby Greek olive
— Crisp olive bread, to serve (optional)

Dirty Martini ²⁰¹⁰

The Dirty Martini can be a great drink, but a lot of olive brines can be really dreadful. Rather than representing the olive flavor, the brine is often simply oily, salty water. I wanted to create a more refined olive taste that would complement the botanicals in gin rather than just dominating its taste with salt. The result is an incredibly subtle, almost creamy olive flavor that really complements the more savory characteristics of a good London dry gin.

1. Combine all the ingredients except the olives in a cocktail tin and stir over cubed ice.

2. Strain and pour into a chilled, small coupette. Garnish with the olives.

INGREDIENTS
— 50 ml (1²/₃ oz) London dry gin
— 15 ml (¹/₂ oz) vermouth
— 10 ml (2 tsp) olive water (page 173)
— 2 green Sicilian olives, to garnish

Dirty Martini

Bloody Mary ²⁰¹⁰

This version of the Bloody Mary is all about isolating the components of the cocktail, creating definitive homemade versions, and putting them all back together again. I love a good Bloody Mary, and I embarked upon an eighteen-month clean-up job that removed all the elements I found to be holding back the drink and enhanced all the best bits.

My pet hate in a Bloody Mary is the gritty texture often produced from including horseradish and pepper granules. I started by redistilling vodka with fresh horseradish using the Rotavapor in order to retain a punchy kick but without the grainy texture. The resulting vodka is pungent and delicious and really shines through the tomato juice, invoking memories of Sunday lunch. People love the stuff, and I often get requests to sell bottles of it to vodka enthusiasts! The pepper granules that are normally ground over the Bloody Mary are replaced by a pepper distillate that integrates perfectly when stirred into the drink. I'm always dissatisfied with the fermented off note that comes from using Tabasco and so I make a hot pepper sauce that retains the slight woodiness of chile along with a real, clean bite of pepper.

Most tomato juices you can find in the supermarket are watery, a dissatisfying result that can also come from fresh-pressing tomatoes. To remedy this problem I mixed equal amounts of nonconcentrated tomato juice and passata (an uncooked sieved tomato puree) for a gratifying tomato taste and consistency. The miso added to the juice provides an umami (savory) quality that really fills the mouth, bolstering the entire drink. It makes sure that the heavier bass notes also stand their ground alongside the high-hitting sharp notes of the horseradish and pepper distillate.

The result is a drink with distinguished components: a clean-tasting Bloody Mary whose flavors hit you at full force but in a linear fashion. Comforting, yet reenergizing!

INGREDIENTS
— 50 ml (1²/₃ oz) homemade horseradish vodka (page 175)
— 15 ml (¹/₂ oz) fresh lemon juice
— 15 ml (¹/₂ oz) Worcestershire sauce
— Pinch of celery salt
— 3 drops of pepper tincture (page 186)
— 3 dashes of hot pepper sauce (page 206)
— 100 ml (3¹/₃ oz) tomato mix (page 165)
— Lemon slice, to garnish

1. Build the ingredients over cubed ice in a highball glass. Beginning with the horseradish vodka, lemon juice, and Worcestershire sauce and finish with the salt and pepper tincture, hot pepper sauce, and finally the tomato mix.

2. Stir and add a lemon slice to garnish.

Bloody Mary

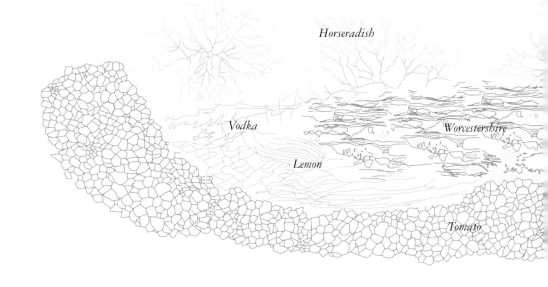

FIGURE 3: Bloody Mary—Flavor and Aroma Journey

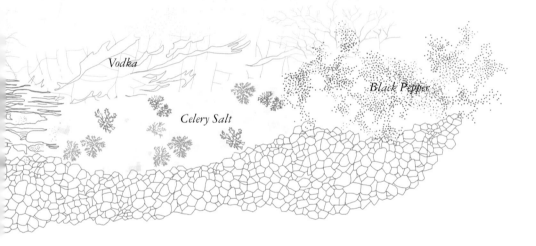

Vodka

Celery Salt

Black Pepper

4.
INSPIRED BY PERFUME

Inspired by Perfume

I find perfume totally fascinating. It possesses a unique multifaceted nature; perfume can be art, alchemy, and commerce—often all at the same time. Reading books on perfumery began as a hobby, sparked by the seductive mix of romanticism and pragmatism inherent to its art. Perfumery is a profession that relies on absolute accuracy, and elements of this can be taken over to cocktails, where making things very precise is essential—simply changing a microliter ($^{1}/_{1000}$ of a milliliter) of an ingredient can make an enormous difference. Our sense of smell is responsible for much of our taste experience, meaning that aroma is a key factor to consider when combining flavors.

The effect of scent on mood and ambience has been well documented over the past ten years. As medicine and psychological techniques have become more advanced, so has our understanding of how the brain interprets odor. I love how, when we smell, the emotion is direct—a message is sent straight to the limbic system of the brain. Books by Mandy Aftel and Luca Turin demonstrate how the working of your nose is interlinked with the way in which flavor works. It is no surprise, then, that a great perfume has the power to awaken emotions, unearth lost memories, and create both an individual and shared nostalgia.

Alchemy is very much like an extended history of alcohol and its production, explaining the preservation of ingredients, flavors, and aromas. The act of the alchemist in the workings of perfumery can parallel those of the bartender in the balancing of a cocktail. They both share the search for the perfect combination, and there are considerable links between flavors and chemicals and how they work together. Combining this knowledge with lengthy Internet research, looking at the chemical structures of ingredients used in cocktail making, I realized the extent of the links between the three disciplines and their shared history. This was of an era before food pairing, and chemical analysis was not readily available, so it was a real learning process.

During this time, Audrey Saunders and I sparked a ten-year dialogue (what we refer to as our linguistic ping-pong across the Atlantic), much of which concerned our mutual passion for aroma. We would lament to one another how aroma is so often overlooked. Audrey made a very poignant comparison with the culinary experience: when we're cooking a stew, the heat releases the aroma of the meat and spices, and accordingly the finished dish appeals to all of our senses. However, within the cocktail domain, save for hot toddies, we rarely use heat to release flavor. For the most part we chill our cocktails with ice, and when you cool something it keeps the aroma within. I wanted to find a way to reawaken the potential of aroma in cocktails but without relying on heat. This chapter explores my foray into the world of the perfumer.

A great perfume has the power to awaken emotions, unearth lost memories, and create both an individual and shared nostalgia.

Blush ²⁰⁰⁶

A turnaround drink for me, Blush was the first cocktail
I created that harmonized years of studying alchemy,
perfumery, and cocktail history. I had always admired
the Hermès perfume house, which often blends rhubarb,
grapefruit, and rose to form the central structure of their
fragrances. These ingredients could be found or replicated
into food-grade essences to make the transition into a
cocktail. I added a rose hydrosol to vodka to replicate the
taste and aroma of roses, and I set about making a homemade
rhubarb cordial that would capture the freshness of English
rhubarb. I then had to decide which delivery system to
use in the cocktail. Rose, rhubarb, and grapefruit share a
chemical combination, and in a lightning-bolt moment of
clarity, I realized that all three ingredients could be both
complemented and amplified by the addition of champagne.

Champagne is served at a slightly higher temperature than
cocktails or spirits, which means that the volatiles carry
well, and the bubbles help by propelling the essences to the
top of the drink, consequently magnifying the flavor. On
paper, the Blush suggests sweetness, but the champagne
elongates the flavors by drying them out. The grapefruit
zest adds an incredible effervescence, and the flavors and
aromas bleed into one another so that, when drinking, you
can't tell where one flavor begins and another ends.

The name "Blush" was initially inspired by the blush of a
rose, but I also like the connotations: it is suggestive both
of an emotional shyness and the blossoming of a rosebud.
In this way we can imagine the flavors of the drink being
teased out and slowly opening up. The languid, relaxed
atmosphere of bars can often promote a certain naughtiness,
which begins internally and slowly makes its way to the
surface, imbuing cheeks with a pink glow. Or perhaps
someone has said something salacious and been caught out.

1. Combine the rose vodka, rhubarb cordial, and Peychaud's
bitters over cubed ice in a cocktail tin and stir.

2. Strain into a chilled coupette or flute. Add the
champagne and a grapefruit twist.

INGREDIENTS

— 25 ml (³/₄ oz) rose vodka
(page 181)

— 15 ml (¹/₂ oz) rhubarb
cordial (page 168)

— 2 dashes of Peychaud's
bitters

— 75 ml (2¹/₂ oz)
champagne

— Grapefruit twist
(page 221), to finish

Blush

Lipstick Rose 2007

I have always been a huge fan of the perfumer Ralf Schwieger for his incredibly conceptual work. Schwieger collaborated with Yves Saint Laurent on his Baby Doll perfume and later worked for Frédéric Malle, with whom he created the fragrance Lipstick Rose, from which this cocktail takes its inspiration.

The Lipstick Rose is named for 1940s femmes fatales, pin-ups, and movie icons, whose images are synonymous with their bold red lipsticks. The lipstick of that generation bears little resemblance to the glosses of today; they were thick, matte lipsticks with the distinct aroma of violets. For me, these are the women who epitomize the cocktail-drinking glamour generation—delivering sassy one-liners before leaving behind only a lipstick imprint on a champagne glass and a waft of their perfume as they saunter off to break another heart. In this way, the Lipstick Rose is an ode to pure attitude.

I didn't want to create a literal translation of the perfume, but rather transcribe the images that are evoked by its scent. This proved far more complex than other perfume-inspired cocktails I had worked on. I had to break down the components that made up the lipstick aroma. I wanted the cocktail to smell as if the perfume were being drunk, yet still allow the drink to have a floral, fruity taste all of its own. I therefore had to create a new balance of the notes directly present in the perfume to translate it into the cocktail format.

I distilled rose petals into a hydrosol (a water-based essence that suspends essential oils inside water) and achieved a raspberry note by using a syrup for a fresh, rather than stewed, note. It was a long search for a violet flavor that was natural and beautiful, but I eventually found a food-grade essence that executed this perfectly. Finally, the zest of grapefruit provided the aroma and oiliness of the perfume's namesake lipstick.

INGREDIENTS

— 15 ml (1/2 oz) rose vodka (page 181)
— 5 ml (1 tsp) raspberry and violet syrup (page 180)
— Dash of Peychaud's bitters
— 100 ml (3 1/3 oz) champagne
— Grapefruit twist (page 221), to garnish
— Homemade lipstick (page 212)

Continues on page 106

Lipstick Rose

Lipstick Rose, continued

I had a rubber stamp made to emulate a full-mouthed pout, and this is pressed into homemade lipstick and imprinted onto the side of the glass. The homemade lipstick is made from carnauba, a natural wax present in most lipsticks, and mixed with food-grade essences that match the violet, rose, and raspberry flavors of the cocktail. The lipstick kiss works as a multifunctional garnish. It seems counter-intuitive to drink through a lipstick mark, but in addition to being a humorous talking point, the lipstick really enhances the flavors of the drink, and the oiliness of the wax mirrors the grapefruit oils that float on top of the cocktail. I really like how this drink functions as a total reversal of what a customer expects from a cocktail.

1. Using a lips-shaped rubber stamp, imprint the lipstick kiss along the rim of a champagne flute or coupette.

2. Pour the rose vodka and raspberry and violet syrup directly into the glass, adding a dash of Peychaud's bitters.

3. Top with the champagne and stir slightly. Finish with a twist of the grapefruit zest and discard.

Gonzales ²⁰¹⁰

Some cocktail ideas are born simply from the drinking habits of friends. My friend Jennifer loved to drink tequila, but over the years I'd become bored with always making her margaritas. The idea behind the Gonzales was to move away from marrying tequila with lime and rather to emphasize the honey and caramel notes found in a reposado tequila. The cocktail originally bore the grand name Armando Torres Gonzales, as the first time Jennifer tried it she claimed it to be reminiscent of her first, sweet-smelling, Mexican lover.

I wanted to use two sweet ingredients that would excite but not overpower the other tequila flavors. I combined mineral water and leatherwood honey to marry woody, earthy notes with a salted caramel liqueur. The honey and caramel float with the lemon—they are complex flavors that complement each other and push each other upward. After visiting Mexico and learning more about the agave plant, and after my study of perfumery, I was able to manipulate this knowledge to really understand and therefore amplify the flavors of this drink. This is how the tuberose honey water, which incorporates tuberose hydrosol, became a late addition to the mix.

A hydrosol is a water-based essence that suspends essential oils inside water. It is an essential ingredient in perfume making because it is an extremely useful way to deliver delicate aroma. An efficient method of making a hydrosol is by using a Büchi rotary evaporator (a Rotavapor). The Rotavapor (see page 160) allows distillation to take place but under a vacuum, so that you are able to change the boiling temperature. This means that delicate ingredients, whose volatiles would normally be destroyed at boiling temperature, can be released.

INGREDIENTS
— 40 ml (1⅓ oz) reposado tequila
— 10 ml (2 tsp) salted caramel liqueur (page 183)
— 5 ml (1 tsp) tuberose honey water (page 172)
— Lemon twist (page 221), to garnish

Continues on following page

Gonzales, continued

Tuberose is a relation of the agave plant, from which tequila is made. The pure essence of tuberose, literally worth its weight in gold, is traditionally used in perfume. It has an incredible sweet, floral scent, somewhat similar to that of honey but with spicy undertones. Using a tuberose hydrosol transformed the Gonzales into a cocktail with incredible depth and sea mless layers. Complex yet drinkable, this is a cocktail that appeals equally to tequila connoisseurs and those with a more hesitant attitude toward the Mexican spirit.

1. Combine all the ingredients except the lemon twist over cubed ice in a cocktail tin and stir.

2. Strain into a small, chilled coupette and finish with a small lemon twist.

Gonzales

The Rose ²⁰¹⁰

For the next step in my perfumery project, I wanted to create a blend of aromas that would result in a unique signature scent rather than replicating an already established perfume. The concept for The Rose was simple: I wanted to re-create the experience of sipping a glass of champagne while walking through an English summer garden. I already knew that rose and champagne worked well together, and I built the other ingredients around this basic structure in order to amplify the depth of the bloom. The champagne couldn't be too heavy—the notes had to be allowed to come through. I talked to my sommelier friend Kelvin, who suggested that Perrier-Jouët, with its delicate, rosy, musky notes, would be a perfect match.

In classical perfumery there are three layers of notes that evaporate at different times once the fragrance has been sprayed. When a perfume lands on skin, the first notes to reach your nose are the delicate and volatile top notes. These top notes consist of small and light molecules. The deeper, more mellow middle notes emerge as the top notes dissipate. The base notes are rich and deep and lingering. I took this perfume pyramid as the structure for how the cocktail would work.

The Rose is all about precision. The food-grade essences are extremely strong and so need to be measured in microliters using a micropipette (see page 158). The essences are mixed with alcohol and put on a sugar cube cut to exactly the same size every time the cocktail is made. The sugar cube aggravates the bubbles, resulting in a surge that propels the aroma right through the cocktail. The carbon dioxide carries and amplifies the aroma and flavor, and as the bubbles split, they release a jet of flavor.

The alcohol works to dissipate the aroma oils by pulling them apart and spreading the aroma, which has previously been trapped in the oil. An ordinary champagne flute traps the aroma, so I use a teardrop flute that holds 100 ml ($3^{1}/_{3}$ oz) of liquid. In this way, the bouquet of the rose opens up, and the three tiers of notes replicate the journey of its bloom. As this

INGREDIENTS
— 1 white La Perruche sugar cube
— 10 microliters of rose essence
— 100 ml ($3^{1}/_{3}$ oz) Perrier-Jouët

cocktail is drunk, an incredible sensory loop develops: aroma follows taste, follows aroma, follows taste, becoming fuller and richer with each sip.

1. Prepare a sugar cube by soaking it in 10 microliters of rose essence, added to it with a pipette.

2. Place the soaked sugar cube in a Riedel grappa glass and top with champagne.

The Rose

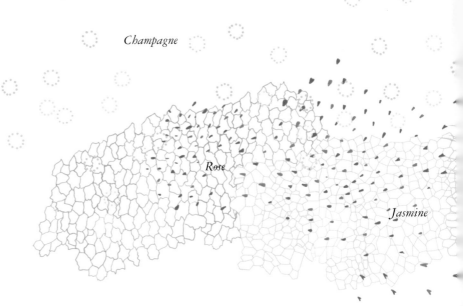

Champagne

Rose

Jasmine

FIGURE 4: The Rose—Flavor and Aroma Journey

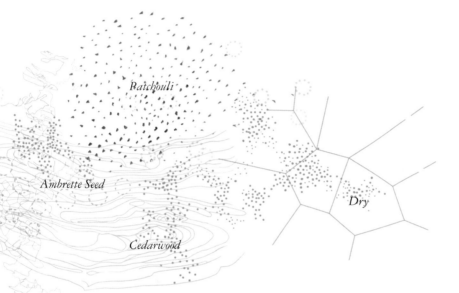

Patchouli

Ambrette Seed

Cedarwood

Dry

Koln Martini 2011

Inspired by a cologne recipe found in the second edition of Jerry Thomas's *Bartender's Guide*, the Koln Martini refigures and modernizes the marriage of perfumery and cocktails by using food-grade essences to create a multilayered spritz. Thomas was the first to galvanize the link between these two crafts. The 1887 edition of his manual showcases how, just as chefs have the ability to work with spice in dry form, bartenders are able to do the same in liquid. In fact, Thomas pioneered the idea of a liquid spice rack by making simple macerations of herbs and spices in alcohol.

With the benefit of technological advances since Thomas's day, the Koln Martini is one of the few perfume drinks I've created that doesn't employ champagne to deliver aroma. The tincture combines petit grain (the distillate of leaves and twigs of the citrus fruit) with vetiver African grass, which produces a salty, green, musky quality. This combination seeks to directly link aroma with the flavors and molecules in gin by identifying and then stripping away its layers. As the notes evaporate at different times they attach themselves to the individual flavors of the gin.

The way in which we taste depends on each molecule's different rate of evaporation. This is dictated by how the molecules are bonded together and consequently how those bonds fall apart. The looser bonds are the ones we taste first, just as in aroma the lightest notes are inhaled first. Each layer of citrus peels off as the drink is consumed. The aroma is ethereal: big on the nose at first but disappearing quickly and playing gently upon the palate. There is, however, real depth to each layer. Using a pipette to deliver the tincture is for both practical and aesthetic reasons. Adding the tincture at the table or bar ensures that the flavor is fresh but also provides an element of theater and a reference to the more rudimentary practices of perfumery.

1. Combine the gin and vermouth in a cocktail tin and stir over cubed ice.

2. Strain into a goblet and add two drops of the Koln tincture. Finish with a cleaned lemon leaf.

INGREDIENTS
— 50 ml (1²/₃ oz) London Dry gin
— 10 ml (2 tsp) dry vermouth
— 2 pipette drops of Koln aromatics (page 190)
— Cleaned lemon leaf, to garnish

Koln Martini

5.
CONCEPT DRINKS

Concept Drinks

The term "concept drink" is a tricky one. It implies a sense of the absurd rather than abstract, of drama as opposed to discreet theater. For me, drinks that have arisen from abstract concepts provide an endlessly interesting way to blur the lines between the craft of bartending, philosophy, art, and science.

What is a bartender doing in a science lab? That is a question I'm asked all the time. My response is always the same: I love to break boundaries! Over the years I have found that the best way to do this is to research—and then utilize—disciplines and methodologies outside the parameters of bartending. Modern bartending is about crafting drinks by stepping out into the world around us, not being limited by the perceived borders of any one profession. This mantra has meant that one of the most important parts of my working life, and perhaps also the most unusual, is the technology and science I use every day at the Drink Factory laboratory.

Ten years of research, borrowing, blagging, and buying have resulted in the lab being full of equipment that most would usually associate with chefs, and even hospitals! My relationship with the first piece of equipment I acquired, the Rotavapor (used to distill a solvent or extract delicate flavors; see page 160), is indicative of my approach to using chemistry to create cocktails. I first saw the Rotavapor used in dessert making by Jordi Roca in Spain and I was transfixed by its accuracy and consistency during the cooking process. The Fat Duck later let me use their Rotavapor and I went wild, putting everything I could through the machine. I spent a long time seeing what I could do with it, exploring its limits. I had to get one for myself! I bought a Rotavapor and it lived in my kitchen for a long time. I quickly learned to record everything— with delicate machinery every nuance makes an incredible difference to the final distillation.

I spent a long time refining processes and methodologies, straying from the manuals and technical brochures, documenting a way to suit working with cocktails. For instance, I often found that an unbalanced result from the Rotavapor created a product that worked really well in cocktails. In fact, I now purposely misuse a lot of my lab equipment.

Eventually my collection of equipment outgrew the kitchen, then outgrew the space upstairs at my bar at 69 Colebrooke Row, and it is now comfortably housed in a fully functioning laboratory nearby. I'm indebted to the lab because it allows me to make a product exactly how I want it, so that I don't have to work constrained by other people's ideas of flavor. It also doesn't have to be complicated: sometimes it's as simple as using a bain-marie rather than spending time hovering over a pan. Equally important is that I can replicate recipes over and over again with incredible accuracy. Consistency is the linchpin of good bartending, but it also helps with the logistics of running a bar—making a business work without compromising creativity. With a functioning lab, all our ingredients are freshly made, polished, and bespoke to our needs.

This profession has afforded me the opportunity to travel extensively, and each time I have visited or revisited a country, I've been able to learn more about philosophies and methodologies that I might not otherwise have encountered. Nearly all of my drinks begin life drawn as a flow chart with signifiers of the initial idea behind the drink, flavor combinations, and possible ingredients. As this chapter explores, concept drinks do not, therefore, pivot purely upon technology but are about inspiration, developing a snippet of philosophy or a lingering line of poetry and translating this into something delicious.

Cocktails are about little moments of time; each drink has a reference point that sparked its creation, and from this a narrative develops. So then you have to figure out how you make science and emotion work together. As this chapter explores, I've found that science can provide the rationale to help release the emotive element of a drink.

Chamomile Cooler

The Chamomile Cooler was the first drink I ever made using a foam, and it remains a favourite to this day. The bottom of the drink is drunk through the foam to release a refreshing hit of both flavors. The cocktail is essentially a whisky sour with a chamomile foam, yet it really gets people talking and changes their expectations of what a cocktail experience can be.

1. Combine all the ingredients except the foam in a cocktail tin and stir over cubed ice.

2. Shake and then strain into a rocks glass.

3. Top with chamomile foam.

INGREDIENTS

— 50 ml (1^1/$_2$ oz) Scotch whisky
— 25 ml (^{3}/$_4$ oz) fresh lemon juice
— 15 ml (^{1}/$_2$ oz) sugar syrup
— Chamomile foam (page 195)

Chamomile Cooler

Prairie Oyster ²⁰⁰⁷

In the film *Cabaret*, Liza Minnelli's character Sally Bowles starts every day with a Prairie Oyster—a spiced, raw egg yolk in brandy, consumed as a hair of the dog. I blended this idea with that classic hangover cure the Bloody Mary to create a concoction that sits in taste, texture, and aesthetics right on the boundary between food and drink.

I spent a long time deconstructing the Prairie Oyster recipe to separate out the flavors, seeking a way to make a clear distinction between each individual component. I adopted a technique that they invented at El Bulli to create a yolk that has a liquid center and a gelatin casing. The tomato juice is frozen in a small round mold shaped just like a natural egg yolk, and this is dipped in gelatin. The gelatin creates a tomato "yolk" that bursts in your mouth. The finely chopped shallots and Kigo shochu mix reference the traditional method of serving oysters.

Serving the cocktail in an oyster shell means that the drink has to be slurped, not sipped, thereby altering your perception of taste and texture. The idea behind this is to change the way the drink is tasted simply by its method of ingestion. By slurping, you pull more air into your mouth, inhaling more oxygen and aerating the flavor, thereby tasting it with your sense of smell. You get an initial hit of pepper sauce, shallots, and Kigo, and when the tomato yolk bursts it releases a clean, vivid, cherry tomato flavor. This counteracts the intensity of the other flavors but then unifies them so that they are wholly refreshing. Using Kigo rather than the more traditional vodka provides the Prairie Oyster with umami—a long-lasting, mouth-watering taste that really fills the mouth.

This recipe takes time but is less complicated than it seems and is a real showstopper. It provides an incredibly different perspective on how a drink can be both consumed and appreciated, blurring the boundaries between food and liquid.

INGREDIENTS

— 400 g (14 oz) cherry tomatoes
— 0.01 g MSK orange food dye
— 1 g vege-gel
— 1 g soy lecithin
— 290 ml (10 oz) Worcestershire sauce
— 25 ml (5 tsp) Kigo shochu
— Dash of raspberry vinegar
— Dash of olive oil
— 5 ml (1 tsp) fresh lemon juice
— Dash of hot pepper sauce (page 206)
— Pinch of finely chopped shallots
— Pinch of celery salt
— Pinch of black pepper

1. To make the tomato juice, slice a tiny incision into the skin of each tomato using a sharp knife. Place the tomatoes in a jug, pour boiling water over them, and leave for 5 minutes before draining. Peel off any remaining skin with your fingers, and briefly blend the tomatoes with an immersion blender. Push the purée through a sieve then spin in a centrifuge, which will clarify the liquid. Add the orange food dye.

2. Pour the tomato juice into a silicone half-sphere mold and freeze overnight. Carefully remove the frozen "yolks" from the mold.

3. Put the vege-gel in a pan with 500 ml (17 oz) of water, heat the solution to 80°C (176°F) and then allow to cool to 55°C (131°F). Check the temperature regularly and if it drops below 45°C (113°F), reheat to 80°C (176°F) and start again.

4. Using a long pin, impale the frozen tomato "yolks" and dip them into the vege-gel twice. It will set instantly, forming a skin around the shape. Place each yolk on waxed paper, and when you have finished dipping them, place them all in the freezer and leave for approximately one hour. As the yolks defrost they become clearer in color and the ice is visibly melted inside. When the center of the yolks are liquid, they are ready to use.

5. Combine the soy lecithin with the Worcestershire sauce and puree with an immersion blender until a foamy consistency. This will make a light and frothy "air" to sit on top of the yolk.

6. Combine the Kigo, vinegar, oil, lemon juice, hot pepper sauce, and shallots in a mixing bowl and stir. Place each egg yolk in an oyster shell and then spoon the Kigo mix over the top, followed by the Worcestershire "air." Season with celery salt and pepper.

Pictured on following pages

Prairie Oyster

Tarragon Caipirinha Ice Pop

Tarragon Caipirinha Ice Pop ²⁰⁰⁸

In life there are party drinks—sugar-loaded syrupy cocktails—and there are drinks that are made for partying. The Tarragon Caipirinha Ice Pop falls into the latter category and was designed as a fun solution to that tiresome problem of dancing and holding your drink at the same time.

Originally made for a cachaça brand in time for a Brazilian-style festival in London, this drink takes a classic caipirinha and subverts it by subtly enhancing the flavor of the sugar cane and using tarragon to produce a cold, tingly sensation on the tongue, which also imbues the mix with a beautiful light-green color. The ice pop style is the perfect accompaniment to some grown-up fun.

1. Combine all the ingredients except the dry ice in a large mixing bowl. Stir vigorously.

2. Pour into ice pop bags and seal with a vacuum, or pour into ziplock bags. Freeze in dry ice, if possible, or in a freezer if not available.

INGREDIENTS

— 1 g tarragon juice (page 163)
— 700 ml (3 cups) cachaça
— 350 ml (1¹/₂ cups) clear lime (page 165)
— 175 ml (³/₄ cup) sugar cane syrup
— 1 liter (4 cups) mineral water
— Dry ice, for freezing

Cosmo Popcorn ^{2005}

Many great food innovations have been discovered entirely by mistake, and this delicious twist on the Cosmopolitan is no exception. While at The Fat Duck's experimental lab, their pastry chef Jockey and I were trying to create a Bellini macaroon by combining a foam with liquid nitrogen. The result was an interesting hard/soft texture, but it didn't quite work for a Bellini. Instead, we created a cranberry-heavy Cosmopolitan and, using a siphon, sprayed it as foam on top of liquid nitrogen. Alarmingly, the frozen foam started to crack and make a popping sound. Eventually it shattered and we scooped out the remains with a spoon. The foam had kerneled and the result looked just like pieces of popcorn. Each bite delivered an incredible cold crunch alongside direct flavor that turned to liquid in the mouth. Since there was no dilution, the full, instantly recognizable flavor of the Cosmopolitan hit you. We made wax paper cones and scooped the Cosmo Popcorn into them, along with plastic ice-cream spoons to devour them with.

The science behind this novelty drink unfortunately results in an utter impracticability for service at a bar. Use of liquid nitrogen should be confined only to the professional kitchen.

1. Add the gelatin sheets to the cranberry juice and heat in a pan until 80°C (176°F) and the gelatin has completely dissolved. Remove from the heat and wait until cool, then combine all the ingredients and place them in an ISI siphon.

2. Charge the siphon with two N$_2$O cartridges and place in the fridge to cool for an hour.

3. Pour some of the liquid nitrogen into a large, stainless-steel, insulated bowl. Remove the siphon from the fridge and, from a safe distance, squirt the cosmo mix at regular intervals into the bowl of liquid nitrogen. Use a wire-mesh skimmer to scoop the popcorn out of the stainless-steel bowl. Repeat with more liquid nitrogen and more of the mix.

4. Scoop into paper ice-cream cones and serve with a flat plastic ice-cream spoon.

INGREDIENTS
— 2 gelatin sheets
— 200 ml (6³/₄ oz) cranberry juice
— 100 ml (3¹/₃ oz) citrus vodka
— 75 ml (2¹/₂ oz) triple sec
— 75 ml (2¹/₂ oz) egg white
— 20 ml (²/₃ oz) fresh lime juice
— 20 ml (²/₃ oz) lime cordial (page 167)
— 10 ml (2 tsp) orange bitters
— 50 ml (1²/₃ oz) sugar syrup

TO SERVE
— Paper ice-cream cones and plastic ice-cream spoons

Cosmo Popcorn

Triple Sec

Sugar

Citrus Vodka

Cranberry

FIGURE 5: Cosmo Popcorn—Flavor and Aroma Journey

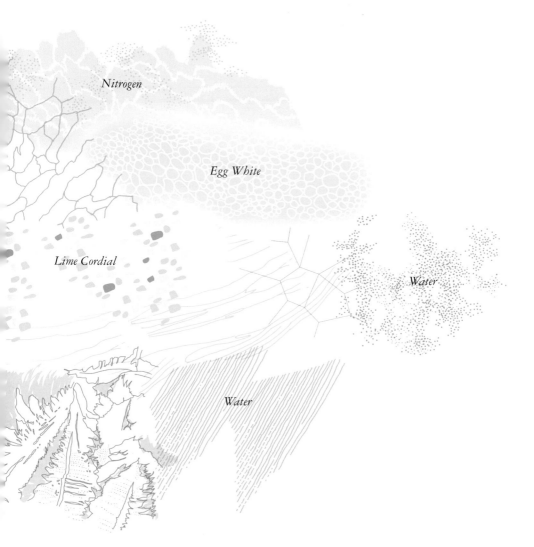

Nitrogen

Egg White

Lime Cordial

Water

Water

Haiku

Haiku ²⁰⁰⁹

The Haiku is all about discreet theater. Influenced by the Japanese notion of working with the seasons, this cocktail is evocative of sitting beneath a cherry blossom tree and was created as a means of demonstrating the idea that however something falls, it falls . . .

The three ingredients used in the Haiku reflect the different components of shochu. Rice water is delicate and incredibly drinkable and makes a direct link to the rice used in the making of shochu. The almond milk draws out the almond notes in Kigo, and the cedar wood also present in the rice milk provides a depth and woodiness that reinforces the concept of whiling away an afternoon languishing beneath a cherry blossom tree.

1. Combine the almond milk rice water and shochu in a cocktail tin and stir over cubed ice.

2. Strain into a small, chilled coupette and serve next to a ramekin of scented cherry-blossom rice paper to be scattered over the finished drink.

Rice Paper Garnish

1. To flavor the rice paper, soak one cotton ball with cherry-blossom essence and cherry-blossom wood essence (both food-grade) and place at the bottom of a jam jar. Cover the cotton with a mesh wire, and sit the rice paper on top.

2. Suspend a cheesecloth bag full of dry rice over the top and seal the jar, allowing the rice paper to absorb the aroma.

3. Leave for at least 2 days, or up to 1 week.

INGREDIENTS
— 20 ml ($^2/_3$ oz) almond milk rice water (page 171)
— 40 ml ($1^1/_3$ oz) Kigo shochu
— White tea–scented cherry-blossom rice paper (see below)

The Morning After the Night Before

Makes four 200 ml (6³/₄ oz) bottles

This drink is inspired by the morning-after ritual of reaching for a glass of water and a tablet to relieve the pain incurred from the previous evening. It's served in a bottle with a tablet on the side, which, when dropped into the glass, carbonates the drink with a dramatic rush of bubbles powering up from the bottom. The concept here is one of action, expectation, and anticipation; when we crack open a can of soda, part of the enjoyment is pulling the tab and hearing the sound of the fizz. This ritual sets up our expectation for the drink.

The drink is reminiscent of a classic Gin Fizz but has been made clear and still. As the bottle is opened there is a disappointing lack of fizz, which goes hand in hand with that deflated morning-after feeling. The "fizz" is found in the tablet sitting alongside the bottle. When the tablet is dropped into the gin it reacts and bubbles, raising the spirits and inspiring a hope for relief from the morning's pains.

1. Mix the water, gin, lemon, and sugar syrup in a pitcher and divide the mix among four bottles.

2. Serve a soda tablet beside each bottle.

INGREDIENTS
— 400 ml (13¹/₂ oz) still mineral water
— 250 ml (8¹/₂ oz) gin
— 125 ml (4¹/₄ oz) clear lemon (page 164)
— 75 ml (2¹/₂ oz) sugar syrup
— 2 g bicarbonate of soda tablet, to serve

The Cocktail Lab | 134 | Tony Conigliaro

The Morning After the Night Before

Silver Mountain 2010

One of the perks of working in the bartending world is being given the opportunity to travel. While designing the menu for the Shochu Lounge, I went back and forth to Japan researching flavors and techniques. In particular I loved picking up some of the soft drinks and types of shochu that weren't available for export. The beautiful six-generation Kyo-ya distillery in Nichinan, Kyushu, became a subject of fascination for me and I visited it many times, building a relationship with the master distiller. It was here that I fell in love with the soft and delicate Kigo.

Dave Broom, friend and spirits expert, once tasted Kigo and remarked that it was like exquisite water. This sparked for me a vision of a Japanese woodland stream, reminiscent of the beautiful river that runs down the mountain next to the distillery. I wanted to emulate the taste of really fresh, cold, spring water—a flavor inextricable from the aroma of its woodland surrounding. I always envisage a running stream as a translucent silver color, implying its movement as it catches the light of the sun or moon; from this image the Silver Mountain was born.

It was never my intention for philosophy to act as the inspiration behind this drink, but it bled its way into all the parameters of a cocktail with such a specific concept. In this way, the image of a silver mountain came first and I built the ingredients around it accordingly. One of the things I like most about Japanese culture and cuisine is the inextricable link between the two. Japanese cooking reflects the natural environment that surrounds it and is quintessentially seasonal. The minimalism of this drink is an intentional reflection of the element of subtraction in Japanese cooking; the best is drawn from what nature gives us, what is unnecessary is removed, and what is most desired is accentuated.

INGREDIENTS

— 50 ml (1 2/3 oz) Kigo shochu
— 25 ml (3/4 oz) silver needle tea (page 172)
— 2.5 ml (1/2 tsp) sugar
— 2 Ruscus leaves, to garnish (see page 220)

Shochu is traditionally drunk with green tea, and I wanted to create a bridge between its traditional service and my woodland concept. The Japanese tea ceremony is a cultural activity involving the ceremonial preparation and presentation of matcha, which is powdered green tea. The tea is made in a minimally adorned room while a poem is read; the room is understated but indicates greater signifiers outside the room. These include an aesthetic of humility, restraint, and simplicity. In this way, the formalities of the ceremony are full of implied meaning. With this in mind, I wanted to create a cocktail that built upon an understated minimalism existing within the framework of a big concept.

I began by working with green tea but found it too overpowering an ingredient for the cocktail format. I liked the idea of jasmine growing by the side of the stream, but again the flavor became more about the tea than the Kigo. It was at this point that I experimented with silver needle tea, which is delicate and has a soft quality to it. I brewed the tea at exactly 70°C (158°F) and let it steep for 5 minutes. Every tea has its optimum brewing point, and it is important not to use boiling water since it can destroy some of the tea's flavor.

To replicate the earthy, woody, and slightly vegetal aroma of a mountain stream I used cassis leaf, which has a gentle sulphur note to it reminiscent of bark, with a "just rained" green scent. This particular sulphur quality reminded me of stones found in and around streams. After playing around with adding sugar, I finally settled on a very minimal quantity. Its purpose is not as a sweetener but rather to give a mouthfeel so that it has a substrata flavor and effect; since the brain doesn't record the flavor, you don't notice the sweetness as a taste but it does register the mouthfeel.

For the garnish, I used Ruscus leaves to imitate the way that leaves fall into a river and are swept along by the running water. As it passes you, a stream gives you a photograph of an instant, of which you catch only one piece. In this way I could imply a sense of history of where the stream has been and where it is going.

1. Combine all the ingredients except the Ruscus leaves in a cocktail tin and stir over cubed ice.

2. Strain and pour into a large, chilled coupette and garnish with the Ruscus leaves.

Plume ²⁰¹⁰

The Plume alludes to elements of the traditional Japanese tea ceremony, aiming to create a sense of space through ritual. There are four principles of the Japanese ceremony: harmony, respect, purity, and tranquillity. This drink makes reference to purity—to be cleansed through the senses. The affila sprig appeals to the sense of sight, sense of touch comes into play when we handle the utensils, sense of smell when we inhale the incense, and sense of taste when drinking the cocktail.

At a Japanese incense "smelling ceremony" I learned a lot about making incense by talking to those who make it professionally. Making my own incense turned into a far nicer project than I'd anticipated—it was very tactile. I'd make a paste of the chosen ingredients with water and then dry it out with a dehydrator. Working with dry aromas rather than liquid ones was a totally new experience for me.

For me, delivering aroma via incense was particularly interesting. The incense is utilized as a way of enhancing flavor in addition to creating a meditative mood. I like the way the idea of aroma is reversed—delivered not inside the drink itself but around it. To create the incense, I identified a series of elements linking back to the drink and ordered them directly from Japan. Using smoke and thinking about how smoke reacts, as opposed to pure aroma or perfume, means that the drink has a completely different delivery. There's something very calming about watching that small plume of smoke circling the drink.

1. Combine all the ingredients in a cocktail tin and stir over cubed ice. Strain into a thimble glass. Serve as follows.

2. Pour the white sand into a small Japanese metal-enameled bowl, leaving a 1 cm (1/3-inch) lip, and brush the sand with a fan brush.

3. Arrange the affila sprig, thimble glass, and incense in a triangle shape in the sand. Light the incense and serve once it starts to smoke.

INGREDIENTS
— 40 ml (1¹/₃ oz) gin
— 20 ml (4 tsp) silver needle tea (see page 172)
— 10 ml (2 tsp) Kigo shochu

TO SERVE
— Handful of white sand
— 1 green tea incense cone (page 210)
— 1 affila sprig (see page 219) or pea shoot

Plume

Kata

Kata [2010]

For centuries, Japanese culture has revered nature as an ideal of beauty. Instead of imposing a man-made concept of beauty on the landscape, nature is synthesized in miniature awe-inspiring gardens. I once visited a beautiful restaurant in Ninchen, Japan, where the entire landscape was manicured according to the seasons in a tradition that dated back to the Emperor's gardens in the 1800s. The result is an incredibly structured composition of nature; the garden blooms in total harmony, each plant carefully worked out for its moment of bloom.

The service of this cocktail is entirely focused on creating a setting using ikebana—the Japanese art of flower arrangement—as inspiration. In addition to the aesthetic, ikebana creates harmony by emphasizing different parts of the arrangement in a minimal way. It is not considered a flower arrangement but rather an arrangement with flowers. In the Kata, the chives are reminiscent of reeds peeking out of water.

The Kata pivots on the flavors of basil and shiso—two herbs from the same family but used in different cultures. The basil and shiso overlap within the drink and work together in an interesting flavor fusion to deconstruct the savory flavors in both the gin and vermouth. The result is herby but delicate, with the slight sweetness of basil playing in the background. Green, aromatic, and lush, to coincide with the herbaceous gin, this drink is about an outward harmony as well as a harmony between neatly interlocking ingredients.

1. Combine the basil gin and shiso dry vermouth in a cocktail tin and stir over cubed ice. Strain and pour into a Japanese bone-china sake cup.

2. Garnish with five rock chives bound with a sixth chive like a daisy chain and shiso cress.

INGREDIENTS
— 40 ml (1^1/$_3$ oz) basil gin (page 202)
— 10 ml (2 tsp) shiso dry vermouth (page 203)
— 6 rock chives and shiso cress, to garnish

Master at Arms ²⁰¹⁰

Although it is true that cocktails have an impressive two hundred–year history, most classic cocktails are American in origin and survivors from a very narrow period of time. It can be hard to break free of this traditional frame of reference, so I spent a long time researching the Georgian period, wondering what ingredients would be available to the discerning Georgian drinker. Britain has a long history as a colonial and seafaring power, and the master at arms is a naval rank referring to an officer responsible for physical training and security on a mercantile ship. He would also often be in charge of doling out rum and port rations. It occurred to me that a stirred rum drink would be an elegant companion to a voyage, Georgian or otherwise!

When it comes to rum cocktails it is very easy to reach for the same flavor combinations. Eliminating the addition of citrus juice transforms the flavor profile of rum in a cocktail and results in a drink miles apart from the fruity rum cocktails I normally work with. The first combination of rum and port proved too sweet and too strong so I set about making a port reduction in the Rotavapor (page 160) so that I could evaporate the alcohol in a very controlled way. Once the port has gone through the Rotavapor it becomes incredibly light; in this way the port reduction can work in the same spirit-to-sweetener ratio as in El Presidente (page 39) or a Manhattan (page 26). The opulent, ruby red of this drink is somewhat of an illusion as the aroma gives way to a rich fruitiness and a pleasing dryness with a surprisingly long finish.

Light and playful, this drink uses technology to bring it to life. The result is very classic and deceptively simple, but the process used to get there is as modern as it gets.

1. Combine all the ingredients in a cocktail tin and stir over cubed ice.

2. Strain and pour into a small, chilled coupette.

3. Tie a small piece of black rope into a sailor's knot around the stem of the glass to serve.

INGREDIENTS
— 50 ml (1^2/$_3$ oz) dark rum
— 20 ml (^{2}/$_3$ oz) port reduction (page 176)
— 5 ml (1 tsp) homemade grenadine (page 182)

TO SERVE
— Black rope, for sailor's knot decoration

Master at Arms

Les Fleurs du Mal

Les Fleurs du Mal ²⁰¹¹

Charles Baudelaire's *Les Fleurs du Mal* (The Flowers of Evil) was published in 1857 and immediately caused public outrage for scaling the terrain of moral corruption, sexual perversion, and alcoholic candor. The volume is a fascinating study of fragrance, intimacy, and ravishing beauty that can be fueled by sin or exist side by side with darkness. Rereading the poem one afternoon, its discussion of the delicate dichotomy between beauty and darkness became the premise for this cocktail.

I love the checkered history of absinthe. Its historical associations are of a banned, evil, and taboo substance, and in France in particular in conjures images of vice. However, in moderate doses, absinthe was allied with inspiration: new views, unique feelings, and a peculiarly clear form of intoxication. A million miles away from the seedy taverns of Paris, absinthe has traditionally been used alongside rose as an ingredient in perfume. This is primarily to extort its fragrant anise and wormwood, but also to release more subtle herbs such as Florence fennel, lemon balm, hyssop, and angelica root.

I wanted to avoid the obvious ways of including absinthe in a cocktail by pairing it with ingredients that were floral, light, and delicate, with the absinthe ominously nestling beside. Essentially a rose sour with a touch of absinthe, Les Fleurs du Mal represents the contest between the two contrasting human impulses toward beauty and darkness.

There are in every man at all times two simultaneous impulses — one toward God, the other toward Satan. (Baudelaire's journal)

1. Combine all the ingredients in a cocktail tin.

2. Dry shake, add cubed ice, and shake again. Strain and pour into a goblet.

INGREDIENTS
— 50 ml (1²/₃ oz) rose vodka (page 181)
— 25 ml (5 tsp) fresh lemon juice
— 25 ml (5 tsp) egg white
— 5 ml (1 tsp) absinthe

Rotavapor

6.

EQUIPMENT & TECHNIQUES

Equipment and Techniques

The equipment housed in my Drink Factory laboratory has been acquired over an eight-year period. During this time, I have not only learned how to use the equipment to obtain incredibly high levels of accuracy but have also invented techniques that manipulate the abilities of each piece of equipment to work uniquely with liquids. This chapter, rather than functioning as a manual as such, explains how I first came to use each piece of equipment and the methods needed for them to work with the liquid format.

Cooking Sous Vide: The Bain-marie & Vacuum Machine

Cooking "sous vide" has been a quiet part of the culinary world for years, but recently its notoriety has begun to snowball, becoming a catalyst for the scientific revolution in the cooking world over the last five years. Bruno Goussault is both a scientist and an economist who gave momentum to the established practice of cooking sous vide, and he's not even a chef—I love that.

For years I had been working in bars making my own ingredients by macerating and infusing fruits and essences into alcohol, often liters and liters at a time. In terms of consistency this can be incredibly problematic; combining natural ingredients with alcohol, especially fruit, always results in a certain amount of natural degradation. Most alcohols have 40 percent alcohol by volume and the remaining 60 percent of water will, over time, affect the flavor of the material. For example, if you put fresh raspberries in gin, eventually a musty flavor will develop as the fruit starts to degrade, tainting the entire batch. The solution to this is cooking sous vide.

Cooking sous vide has two distinct parts: sealing ingredients in a bag in a vacuum machine and then cooking them in a bain-marie, which provides a precise regulation of heat. These two pieces of equipment are a dream team: together you have complete control over your ingredients, extracting flavor in an incredibly precise way with satisfying, flavorful results. The sous vide bag works as a hermetic seal, keeping in both juices and aroma; and by cooking in water you get better heat transfer than you would in an oven. Sous vide liquids can be served in drinks immediately, but using this method for batch cooking makes the preparation for the bar, or for a party, really practical.

It's crucial to select the correct water temperature for the bain-marie. Finding the perfect time and temperature to achieve the exact results I want often involves a long series of trial and error. I time all my infusions or macerations and meticulously record them in a log book with their corresponding temperatures.

For those who don't have commercial sous vide equipment, it can be replicated at home using simple kitchen items—see page 151.

Step-by-step sous vide

1. Prepare the ingredients.

2. Vacuum-pack.

3. Set temperature for cooking.

4. Cook for a set time in a bain-marie.

5. Rest or cool.

Bain-marie

I first used a bain-marie at Roka in 2005 and it truly revolutionized the way that I was able to make bespoke ingredients. Water baths, or bain-maries, are thought to have originally been created by an alchemist named Maria the Jewess and were devised to control a slow rise in temperature using boiling water. Centuries later, their purpose and function has not really changed.

How it works

1. Place the product into a plastic bag.

2. Vacuum-seal the bag.

3. Release the vacuum.

4. Cook for a set time at a set temperature in the bain-marie.

I'm a huge fan of this self-contained method of cooking; carefully controlling a gentle heat slowly releases the flavor, and since there is no oxidation and nowhere for the flavor to escape to, this preserves the natural, delicate flavors that are easily destroyed through heat. One of the biggest advantages we have in modern water baths is that we are able to regulate the temperature to a very specific degree. This allows you to really get the best from the ingredients, ensuring that even very delicate volatiles, such as flowers, are not destroyed during the cooking process.

In addition, cooking ingredients at a low temperature, for longer, bonds the flavors in a more subtle way. The result is an unparalleled smoothness. The water is rotated so that it is always at a constant temperature. This way the heat reaches every part of the ingredient, gently extracting its flavor. This style of cooking is executed with incredible efficiency and consistency.

Vacuum Machine

The vacuum machine has been used for years to preserve food and liquid and enhance their storage life. By sucking all the air (and therefore oxygen) away from a product, vacuum-packing simultaneously forestalls the two biggest causes of food degradation: direct oxidation and aerobic microbial growth. Consequently, the technology substantially increases shelf life and therefore is incredibly practical for preparation purposes.

It may seem unnatural to store liquid in a plastic bag, but vacuum-sealing protects whatever is inside the bag during the cooking process. In addition to the economic value, because everything stays within the bag there is nowhere for the flavor to escape to. We tend to associate the kitchen with the smell of good cooking, but in the lab, even though we cook delicious ingredients sous vide all the time, it only ever smells of whatever perfume I've been tinkering with. This is because all of the aroma from the food becomes trapped in the bag. The final product is full of flavor; it smells fantastic, and the fully humid environment inside the bag eliminates drying, which means it's juicy too.

The vacuum machine is the real linchpin behind the practicability of all the other pieces of equipment I use in the lab. One of the first to use the vacuum machine in a bar, I find it absolutely invaluable for preparing and later storing ingredients until they're needed.

How it works

The ingredients or liquids are placed in plastic bags. These are then laid in the chamber, with their open ends on a sealing bar. After the lid is closed, a powerful vacuum pump evacuates the air. The sealing bar heats up, melting a strip of the bag and bonding it closed. The chamber then returns to atmospheric pressure and unlocks the lid.

1. Fill the bag over a cylinder (a large glass or cocktail shaker, for example) to make it easier to fill without spilling.

2. Set the vacuum level and sealing times on the machine.

3. Place the bag in the chamber. Laying the bag on a ramp will help prevent it from leaking during the sealing process.

Additional benefits

It's a basic bit of equipment, but the vacuum machine can also be used to do incredible things that it's not supposed to do. For example, I discovered that I could flavor different fruits not just by putting liquid alongside them in the bag, but by adding it outside the tray. When I was experimenting with the garnish for the Somerset Sour, I was using a melon baller to scoop apple balls, which are very porous and have lots of air and juice in them. Placing these in a tray with a liquid around it (pectin and grass flavor), without a bag, causes the vacuum to pull the juice and air out of the apple. When you turn the machine off, the chamber refloods and the air rushes back in, forcing the liquid on the tray into what used to be the air cells in the apple. It works just like squeezing a sponge. This modifies the texture of the fruit, so that it is at once juicier and yet crisper—and a truly fantastic garnish! You can do this with any porous fruit that isn't too fibrous.

Cooking Sous Vide at Home

Sous vide technology is becoming more accessible and more affordable, but all recipes that call for sous vide cooking can be replicated at home. Before I could justify buying a bain-marie for myself, I began experimenting with ziplock bags in pans with thermometers. Water is a better medium for heat transfer than the air in the oven, and a far more precise temperature is reached than could be achieved with a pan on the burner. Although labor-intensive, it is a really effective way of getting flavor into alcohol, as well as quicker and more consistent than infusions or macerations.

To re-create a bain-marie at home, all you need is two saucepans, one smaller than the other. Pour water into the larger pan, place the smaller one within the larger one, also filled with water, and heat on the stove. You can regulate and monitor the temperature using a thermometer to make sure that the temperature is constant. Just make sure you fine strain your final product.

The vacuum machine can also be improvised. To re-create a vacuum bag, there are a couple of options. You can either buy a cheap sealing unit, which will do an adequate job, or, if you are feeling adventurous, you can place a straw into the center of the bag, wrap a rubber band around the top, and suck the air out of the bag manually. It might sound silly, but it will get the job done.

Centrifuge

One of the earliest centrifuges was made by Antoni Pranotti in 1864, which at the time was used to separate milk from fat in the production of dairy products. A centrifuge works on the sedimentation principle: it uses centrifugal force to separate parts of a mixture that have different densities. This causes liquids of a medium weight to become sandwiched between the denser, heavier liquids that fall to the bottom of the container and the lighter liquids that remain at the top. Centrifuges are widely used in medical and scientific labs, but the idea of having a centrifuge behind a functioning bar or in a restaurant kitchen is probably something still quite alien to most!

The primary purpose of the Drink Factory's centrifuge is to clarify liquid. Color molecules in liquid are among the largest, and the bigger the molecules are, the harder your saliva needs to work in order to break down flavor. If the color molecules are removed, a more immediate and deeper flavor comes through. Clarified products tend to have a different mouth-feel from nonclarified products since the elements that usually make them cloudy have been removed. The mouthfeel is lighter and smoother, and consequently the final result is a cleaner taste. For example, clarified rhubarb makes for an incredible cordial; rhubarb is naturally very fibrous, so I cook the fruit until soft enough to release its flavor, then centrifuge it to remove the pesky fibers that interfere with its flavor. The resulting juice tastes clean and bright without compromising the delicious sweet-tart combination of the fruit.

In addition to having an improved mouthfeel, clarified liquid looks fantastic! Serving up a completely clear tomato juice, for example, is an interesting twist that challenges both aesthetic and taste preconceptions. It was at Isola in 1999 that I first began playing around with the idea of clarifying in order to make a Bloody Mary Martini. The idea was to serve vodka stirred with a totally clear tomato juice, using an ice cube frozen with spices that melted as the drink was stirred. The result was often a complete surprise to the customers—a really striking effect that got people talking.

Before I acquired a centrifuge, to make the clear tomato consommé I would have to cook the tomatoes and gently peel off their skin. The skinless tomatoes would be puréed, mixed with a agar-agar (a gelatin derived from seaweed), and then hung in cheesecloth in the fridge overnight. Color molecules are bigger than flavor molecules, so by force of gravity the heavier color molecules slowly drip through the cheesecloth, leaving behind an incredibly flavorful, but totally clear, tomato consommé. In addition to this taking some time, I found that the flavors and aromas of the fridge crept their way into the tomatoes. Using a centrifuge eliminates the aroma problem and produces a superior and more efficient product in just ten minutes!

The first centrifuge I played around with was borrowed and lived in my kitchen for six months. I spent a long time tinkering with different speeds and angles (as the angle moves out, the greater the centrifugal force). Such lengthy experimentation had the added bonus of being great for my health as I spent this time drinking endless quantities of fresh, clarified juice! It was a logical step to buy a centrifuge for use at the bar, and I purchased my first one in 2009. It completely revolutionized the way I made juice in a commercial environment—I can now make juice in batches and use the vacuum machine to store the product in the fridge. More efficient, cleaner, and producing much less waste than any other option, the centrifuge is imperative to the organization of my lab. If you make a lot of juices in a bar or restaurant, it will pay for itself very quickly.

Soxhlet Still

In 2005 I was experimenting with extracting flavor from bark and fairly hard spices to use in my own bitters. Since I couldn't afford a vacuum at this time, the Soxhlet still was a great way to try out ideas. This still works using an evaporation loop; it evaporates, condenses, and evaporates again for as long as is needed. If I put a harder ingredient through the still, such as star anise, I can siphon the oil off the top using a needle. However, this can be quite a long process, taking up to four hours at a time.

Vacuum distillations are more precise, but if you don't have the budget for a Rotavapor, then this is a really good way to start doing things. You can add a vacuum to this still, but that can make it a little tricky to use.

Büchner Funnel with Vacuum Pump

Looking through scientific equipment catalogues in 2006, I came across the Büchner—a fantastic system for filtration. Used when making macerations or infusions, it produces a cleaner product by filtering out the extraneous bits of a maceration (residue, powder, and fibers), essentially arresting the flavor so that it doesn't keep aging or change flavor profile over time. Rather than waiting for these residues to drip through, the force of the pump pushes them; this speeds up the entire process, and the resulting product will mellow only marginally. I started by using an aquarium pump attachment to provide the vacuum, but soon moved onto the more powerful vacuum pump, which creates a vacuum faster.

The Büchner funnel is a really simple way to make a cleaner and, most importantly, more stable product.

Getting the best out of the Büchner funnel

1. Put the vacuum hose onto the collection chamber.

2. Place the Büchner funnel into the rubber bung at the top of the collection chamber.

3. The choice of filter paper to insert is important. For bigger flavors you want to get more of the liquid out and so need filter paper with bigger micron filters; smaller particles need smaller papers. Filters come in paper and cellulose.

4. Put the liquid you want to filter into the Büchner funnel and turn the vacuum on—this will suck the liquid through, leaving the residue behind.

Microjuicer

The microjuicer is the king of juicers. Fantastic for juicing really fine ingredients such as lemongrass and ginger, a microjuicer effectively removes all the fibers that get in the way of a clean, refined juice. Attachments to make oil are available so that you can retrieve the oils from whatever you put through. These can then be mixed with water so that you can use them later to make hydrosols or your own essential oils.

Induction Heater

An induction heater works using an electromagnet through which an alternating current is passed. Gas will always fluctuate, so rather than heating ingredients over a naked flame, we use an induction heater every day in the lab to achieve an even heat distribution with consistent and accurate temperatures. I've had one of these the height of practicality, since about 2004 when I first saw pastry chefs using them. Induction heaters are really useful because you can carry them around; this is great for events when I need a heat source outside of the bar or kitchen as it means I don't have to use a dangerous heat source like gas or electric. It makes the process much smoother.

Cold Smoker & Smoke Gun

Smoky notes in flavor are complex and give a real depth and a new dimension to whatever they are combined with. The cold smoker is more of a unit as opposed to a machine. It allows you to construct an extension to a grill or smoker so that by the time the smoke gets into the actual chamber it's completely cool. With the smoke cold, you can put things such as fresh fruit in there and smoke them without altering their structure. I first did this with cherries to garnish a Manhattan; deceptively, they appear to be fresh pitted cherries, but once bitten, a slight smokiness is released, and in turn this gives an amazing new angle to a Manhattan.

Smoked syrups, which can introduce an interesting and multifaceted element to any cocktail, can be simply made with the help of a smoke gun. First you make a smoked sugar by sealing sugar granules in a ziplock bag and snaking the tube of the smoke gun inside. Once the smoke has filled the ziplock bag, pull the tube out and close the bag until the smoke dissipates and is completely absorbed into the sugar. This smoky sugar can then be used to make a syrup simply by adding water.

Dehydrator

Essentially, a dehydrator is a basic way to draw out moisture from ingredients. It works by blowing hot air through a system of different tiers—like a giant hairdryer but on a lower heat. The heat source can be adjusted according to how slowly you want dehydration to occur; for example, slow dehydration is necessary for more delicate volatiles, and a by-product of this method is that it also preserves them.

The dehydrator is fantastic for getting the best out of a multitude of more esoteric ingredients, exposing the full range of their flavor profile. When exploring the flavor profile of nettles for the Nettle Gimlet (page 68), for example, I found that although fresh nettles have a minty quality, by dehydrating them I could extrapolate more tannic and tea-like notes from the nettle. So I cut the leaves and spread them evenly across the tiers on a low heat, leaving them for a few hours to dry out while occasionally rotating the tiers to get an even dryness. Once brewed for use in the cordial, the flavor from the nettles was incredible!

Acquiring a dehydrator also totally changed the way I could work with garnishes. In 2009, I was working on the first version of The Rose (page 110), which I wanted to garnish with rose petals. The only way I could envisage executing this was to dry out the petals so that they wouldn't shrink and wither. Using the dehydrator meant that I could preserve the delicate petals and later go on to infuse them with a rose tincture so that the aroma of the flower could float up from the glass. In addition to expanding my repertoire of garnishes, the water content of food can often be quite high, so using a dehydrator results in a fantastic, more concentrated flavor. This is particularly useful for making purées for savory cocktails. I've found that drying out tomatoes meant that more "umami" could be extracted from the fruit, and this resulted in a richer flavor that could then be used in a homemade passata.

The drawbacks of the dehydrator are that it can take a long time and you have to be really careful with delicate ingredients to make sure they don't become stuck to the ring inside. When dehydrating, the hot air rises from the bottom, so it's also a good idea to rotate the rings now and again so that the material at the bottom doesn't dehydrate too fast.

Separatory Funnel

The separatory funnel is a fantastic bit of equipment because it can separate two liquids with different densities—an extremely useful tool when making hydrosols. In contrast to alcohol-based oils, which can interfere with the structure of the drink, water-based hydrosols are perfect for introducing subtle flavors in cocktails. The first hydrosol I ever made was jasmine and I used it in a delicious rice-based cocktail in 2009. I was astonished by how quickly I could achieve fantastic results. It's incredibly simple: just pour your chosen two liquids into the funnel, and as the lighter liquid floats to the top it flavors the more dense liquid as it passes. For example, to make a mint hydrosol:

1. Combine mint oil with mineral water.

2. Shake vigorously.

3. Pour into the funnel.

4. Wait while the oil gradually floats to the top; as it does it will flavor the water.

5. Turn the valve and siphon off the water below, leaving the oil at the top.

Depending on the oils and how much flavor you want, you can use this method to make a really punchy hydrosol by leaving the two liquids for longer, or a lighter hydrosol by leaving them for a shorter amount of time.

Heat Stirrer

The heat stirrer is really useful for mixing together ingredients with a constant, permeating temperature. It has a heated glass panel on the top and a magnetic beam that spins around so that it can heat consistently without need for manual stirring. When I first started working with fine gelatin in 2006, I found the heat stirrer to be invaluable. Gelatin is comprised of a series of protein chains; to open them up they need a constant heat source as well as agitation. If you simply tried to heat gelatin over an induction heater, the material at the bottom would open up in one lump, but when stirred constantly, all the protein chains open up simultaneously, and this ensures that the gel has no lumps.

Micropipette

Essential oils are an integral ingredient in many of my cocktail recipes. I first started to explore their potential when researching how perfumers put together their scents and realized just how intensely accurate you had to be. These oils are comprised of highly concentrated flavors and, consequently, using micropipettes—which measure to $^1/_{1000}$ of a milliliter—is the only way to accurately control your effect on the overall flavor of a product. It lends an unparalleled level of precision to using essential oils—squidgy pipettes just don't hack it!

The micropipettes are used every day in my lab to compound fragrances and to make bar prep more efficient by adding essences directly into their respective bottles: dry essence tincture (page 186) to dry vermouth, cassis into silver needle tea (page 172), lime to cachaça. They also lend the lab an air of CSI.

Homogenizer

A homogenizer is a machine that transforms the consistency of a substance by breaking up its particles, resulting in a more uniform, or homogenous, product. There are several types of homogenizer used in the food industry and in science laboratories, but the one we use in the Drink Factory lab is a simple model that works using a series of fast-spinning sharp blades. I use this tool for every fresh juice that I make, especially for more fibrous juices such as lemon, lime, and rhubarb. When the blades spin, they break up the fibers of the juice, which produces a rounder, fuller, richer flavor. There are different levels on the homogenizer so that you can choose the speed at which the blades spin. The more fibrous the juice, the higher the level needed. However, be careful not to homogenize a juice for too long at too high a speed, or it will begin to burn. The homogenizer is incredibly useful when making batches of juice because it reduces the variance between each batch.

Refractometer

The refractometer is a handheld device that I use to measure the concentration of alcohol levels. It works along the principle of refraction—measuring the degree to which light changes direction when passing through a liquid.

It is incredibly useful to know the exact alcohol percentage of my cocktails so that I can truly understand how they work. I started making homemade liqueurs in 2008, and to ensure consistency of product I bought a basic refractometer with a glass slider. Later I moved on to an electronic one, which is more accurate and easier to read with darker liquids. Later, when I first started distilling using the Rotavapor, I had to make sure that the ABV (alcohol by volume) of the distillate was at 40 percent rather than the 70 percent at which it first comes off. To lower it, I add water until it reaches the desired level on the refractometer. It's an essential piece of equipment for ensuring accuracy.

Thermomix

The Thermomix is the ultimate blender—with titanium blades, it is incredibly powerful and can blend any number of hard ingredients into a superfine powder. Powders are useful because they have more surface area, which means more flavor can be extracted from the product. I've used the Thermomix for making powders from bits of barrel stave or nutmegs, and without a doubt the fresher the powder the more flavorful the product.

The Thermomix is also incredibly efficient because it has a heating element. This allows you to make purées by combining your ingredients directly in the Thermomix, then simply setting the heat and letting it spin. The resulting blend is fantastic because it cooks consistently as it rotates. Temperature control means that you can keep a drink in it at a very specific temperature and serve it straight out of the Thermomix—so practical and accurate!

Brix Meter

The Brix meter is a small, usually handheld device for measuring the amount of sugar in liquids or fruits—the bigger the sugar crystals, the higher the reading. Brix meters are extensively used in the wine-making industry and by farmers for testing the sugar content of grapes, fruit, and vegetables to help determine the best time for their harvest. This ensures that the products reach consumers in their most perfect state or that they are ready for the process of vinification.

There are a couple of different types of Brix meter; I first purchased a basic model in 2008 that had a glass slider, but soon moved on to an electronic one with a laser that refracts off the glass plate. In addition to being more accurate, it also allows me to measure brown spirits, which had previously been hard to get a reading from as their color obscured the plate.

I use the Brix every day to test syrups, cordials, purées, and liqueurs so that I achieve the same results every time. I also use the Brix each time we cook fruit and spirits sous vide. The sugar content in fruit is a major factor in the final flavor, and consequently I test each box—fruits harvested at different times of the year, or from different regions, vary wildly, affecting the outcome of the infusion and any cocktail that they may later be used in. We use sugar as an ingredient in cocktails so often without really knowing much about its effect. The more information we have about cocktails, the better we can understand how they work. The Brix meter is a truly worthwhile investment if you are making your own ingredients, probably the most important bit of equipment in which I've ever invested!

Rotavapor

The Rotavapor is an instrument used to distill a solvent. The purpose of distillation is to separate a given mixture into its components based on their respective volatilities, through the process of evaporation and condensation. What makes the Rotavapor so fantastic is that it has a vacuum. This allows you to evaporate things at lower boiling points because you're evaporating through pressure rather than heat. This is incredibly useful because the less heat you use, the less likely you are to damage or pull apart the more delicate volatiles of an ingredient. Alcohol is a fantastic medium for carrying flavor and volatile aromas. You can extract the purest and freshest flavors from ingredients by removing the water and replacing it with a solvent such as alcohol, gently and at low temperatures. This means your final product has a fuller spectrum of aroma and flavor notes.

The rotation of the evaporating flask, immersed in a heated water bath, increases the surface area of the product, greatly speeding up distillation and also, through forced convection, keeping the mixture evenly mixed and heated, to promote stable, even evaporation. For example, when distilling rose petals, you have very delicate, small molecules, which too much heat would simply burn. With less heat, the delicate molecules are preserved and come through along with the bigger molecules. In this way you have the big picture of what a rose is. What I love about the Rotavapor is that it is one of the most complicated pieces of equipment used in the lab but the products made from it are incredibly poetic.

Chiller

The chiller is an attachment that I employ every time the Rotavapor is used. This tool reduces the temperature of the coils in the Rotavapor distillation, which means that it condenses the evaporating liquid more efficiently—the lower the temperature, the better the condensation, otherwise the mixture begins to evaporate out. It's like a cat-and-mouse game with volatiles—the trick is to not let the small molecules get away so that as much as possible of the whole flavor comes through. The difference between the distillations with and without is remarkable!

Peristaltic Pump

A good friend of mine, Dave Arnold, is the head of the food technology department at the French Culinary Institute, New York. The peristaltic pump is an attachment to the Rotavapor that he rigged up for us at the Drink Factory. One of the problems that occurs the first time you distill an ingredient that you've not tried before is that you don't know where to cut (stop) the distillation. The peristaltic pump allows me to cut the heads and tails from the Rotavapor vacuum still without breaking the seal and thereby losing an enormous amount of volatiles. This allows you to pull off parts of the ingredient to see where the best concentration of flavors are, without compromising the final flavor of the distillation.

7.
JUICES

Fresh juices are imperative to the cocktail formula. Freshly pressed always tastes better: by preparing juices *à la minute,* or as close to service as possible, the flavor is more natural and more intense. All fresh juices quickly lose their potency and impact, even if they are bottled and sealed in the fridge, so whether I'm using the juice for service in the bar or at home, I never keep the bottle for more than twenty-four hours. Once the juices are pressed I use a homogenizer to give a cleaner edge to the flavor, but this is an optional extra for the following recipes.

Orange & Clementine Juice

Yield: 500 ml (17 oz)

1. Remove five pieces of zest from the oranges.

2. Juice the oranges and clementines respectively—aim for 100 ml (3½ oz) of clementine juice and 400 ml (14 oz) of orange juice.

3. Express the oils from the orange zest by twisting the slices over the juice.

4. Homogenize the juice in four 20-second blasts.

INGREDIENTS
— 6 organic oranges
— 10 organic clementines

EQUIPMENT
— Knife
— Chopping board
— Juicer
— Homogenizer

Pink Grapefruit Juice

Yield: 400 ml (14 oz)

1. Remove five slices of zest from the grapefruits, avoiding the pith.

2. Slice the grapefruits in half and juice them.

3. Express the oils from the zest by twisting the slices over the juice.

4. Homogenize the juice in four bursts of 25 seconds.

5. Add the nootkatone using a micropipette and stir to mix.

INGREDIENTS
— 8 large organic
   pink grapefruits
— 5 microliters of
   nootkatone

EQUIPMENT
— Knife
— Chopping board
— Juicer
— Homogenizer
— Micropipette

Tarragon Juice

Yield: 1 g

1. Put the tarragon through a microjuicer.

2. Strain using a Superbag.

INGREDIENTS
— 30 g (1 oz) fresh tarragon

EQUIPMENT
— Microjuicer
— 100-micron Superbag

Broiled Lemon Juice

Yield: 100 ml (3 1/2 oz)

1. Chop the lemons in half and broil at medium heat until golden brown.

2. Juice the broiled lemons.

3. Strain using a Superbag.

4. Homogenize in four 25-second bursts.

INGREDIENTS
— 5 Sicilian lemons

EQUIPMENT
— Knife
— Chopping board
— Broiler
— Juicer
— 100-micron Superbag
— Homogeniser

Clear Lemon

Yield: 300 ml (10 oz)

1. Heat 125 ml (4 1/4 oz) of the lemon juice with the agar-agar in a pan on the induction heater at 95°C (203°F).

2. Stir until the agar-agar dissolves.

3. Take off the heat, add the remaining 250 ml (8 1/2 oz) of lemon juice, and whisk together.

4. Seal the juice in a vacuum bag and place in the freezer overnight.

5. Once frozen, remove from the freezer and place the block of frozen juice in a funnel lined with a coffee filter and allow to defrost in a jug. The clear juice will drip through as the block melts.

6. Strain with a Superbag.

INGREDIENTS
— 375 ml (12 3/4 oz) fresh lemon juice
— 0.7 g agar-agar

EQUIPMENT
— Measuring pitcher
— Small scales
— Pan
— Induction heater
— Whisk
— Vacuum machine and bag
— Funnel
— Coffee filter
— Jug
— 100-micron Superbag

Clear Lime

Yield: 300 ml (10 oz)

1. Heat 125 ml (4¹/₄ oz) of the lime juice with the agar-agar in a pan on the induction heater at 95°C (203°F).

2. Stir until the agar-agar dissolves.

3. Take off the heat and add the remaining 250 ml (8¹/₂ oz) of lime juice, and whisk together.

4. Seal the juice in a vacuum bag and place in the freezer overnight.

5. Once frozen, remove from the freezer and place the block of frozen juice in a funnel lined with a coffee filter and allow to defrost in a jug. The clear juice will drip through as the block melts.

6. Strain with a Superbag.

INGREDIENTS
— 375 ml (12³/₄ oz) fresh lime juice
— 0.7 g agar-agar

EQUIPMENT
— Measuring pitcher
— Small scales
— Pan
— Induction heater
— Whisk
— Vacuum machine and bag
— Funnel
— Coffee filter
— Jug
— 100-micron Superbag

Tomato Mix

Yield: 2 liters (8¹/₂ cups)

1. Make a paste of the barley miso by adding the tablespoon of water.

2. Mix with the tomato juice and passata until the miso paste has completely dissolved.

INGREDIENTS
— 20 g (³/₄ oz) barley miso
— 1 tbsp mineral water
— 1 liter (4¹/₄ cups) organic tomato juice
— 1 liter (4¹/₄ cups) passata

EQUIPMENT
— Large scales
— Tablespoon
— Mixing bowl

8.
CORDIALS

●

Homemade cordials are an important method of control for bartenders, who at all times must be considering the balance of their drink. By making your own cordial you can complement the flavor profile of all your drink's ingredients; this way you are not just using what you have at hand, but tailor-making a key ingredient. I have often thought it to be a bad bartending mentality to use only what is commercially available when it comes to cordials—this is not a practice that you would see employed by chefs, who always seem to be seeking veracity and control of their ingredients. All cordials will keep for up to three weeks in sealed glass bottles.

Lime Cordial

Yield: 1.9 liters (8 cups)

1. Combine the sugar and mineral water in a pan and bring to a boil on an induction heater.

2. Take off the heat and add the lime zest and juice.

3. Check that the Brix reading is 35 and slowly increase the sugar if it is lower.

4. Add the citric acid and tartaric acid.

5. Chill in an ice bath for 24 hours, then strain using a Superbag.

6. Bottle and store in the fridge.

INGREDIENTS
— 450 g (1 pound) sugar
— 1.14 liters (4³/₄ cups) mineral water
— 10 g (¹/₃ oz) lime zest
— 480 ml (17 oz) fresh lime juice
— 14.25 g (¹/₂ oz) citric acid
— 5.4 g tartaric acid

EQUIPMENT
— Large and small scales
— Measuring pitcher
— Pan
— Induction heater
— Brix meter
— 100-micron Superbag
— Glass bottle

Gooseberry Cordial

Yield: 1.1 liters (4³/₄ cups)

1. Combine the gooseberry juice, mineral water, and sugar in a pan.

2. Heat over an induction heater and bring the sweetness to 35 on a Brix meter.

3. Take off the heat and add the malic and tartaric acids.

4. Bottle and store in the fridge.

INGREDIENTS
— 375 g (13¹/₄ oz) gooseberry juice
— 375 g (13¹/₄ oz) mineral water
— 250 g (8³/₄ oz) caster sugar
— 5 g malic acid
— 2.2 g tartaric acid

EQUIPMENT
— Large scales
— Jug
— Pan
— Induction heater
— Brix meter
— Small scales
— Glass bottle

Rhubarb Cordial

Yield: 1.4 liters (6 cups)

1. Dice the rhubarb into bite-sized pieces and separate into three batches.

2. Place in vacuum bags and cook for 1 hour at 60°C (140°F) in a bain-marie. Squeeze the bags in the middle of the process to break the veins of the rhubarb and release the flavors.

3. Blend the cooked rhubarb with the water in the Thermomix, then place in a centrifuge and spin at 5000 rpm for 10 minutes. Strain using a Superbag until only approximately 480 ml (2 cups) of juice is left.

4. Heat the juice along with the sugar in a pan over an induction heater. Bring the sweetness to 35 on a Brix meter.

5. Add the malic acid.

6. Bottle and store in the fridge.

INGREDIENTS
— 1.1 kg (1 pound 5 oz) trimmed fresh rhubarb
— 1 liter (4¼ cups) mineral water
— 450 g (1 pound) superfine baker's sugar
— 10 g (⅓ oz) malic acid

EQUIPMENT
— Knife
— Chopping board
— Large scales
— Measuring pitcher
— Vacuum machine and bags
— Bain-marie
— Thermomix
— Centrifuge
— 100-micron Superbag
— Pan
— Induction heater
— Brix meter
— Glass bottle

Elderflower Cordial

Yield: 1.15 liters (4³/₄ cups)

1. Combine the sugar and mineral water in a pan and bring to a boil on the induction heater.

2. Take off the heat and add the lime zest and elderflowers.

3. Check that the Brix reading is 35 and increase the sugar if not.

4. Add the citric acid and tartaric acid.

5. Chill in an ice bath for 24 hours, then strain using a Superbag.

6. Bottle and store in the fridge.

INGREDIENTS
— 450 g (1 pound) sugar
— 1.14 liters (4³/₄ cups) mineral water
— 10 g (¹/₃ oz) lime zest
— 100 g (3¹/₂ oz) fresh elderflowers
— 14.25 g (¹/₂ oz) citric acid
— 5.4 g tartaric acid

EQUIPMENT
— Large and small scales
— Measuring pitcher
— Pan
— Induction heater
— Brix meter
— 100-micron Superbag
— Glass bottle

Nettle Cordial

Yield: 1.14 liters (4³/₄ cups)

1. Combine the sugar and mineral water in a pan and bring to a boil on an induction heater.

2. Add the nettle leaves to the water and stew for 10 minutes or until the water becomes golden. Be very careful not to burn or overcook the nettles. The result should be a light straw color.

3. Check that the Brix level is 35 and increase the sugar if not.

4. Add the citric acid and tartaric acid.

5. Strain through a Superbag and bottle. Store in the fridge.

INGREDIENTS
— 450 g (1 pound) superfine baker's sugar
— 1.14 liters (4³/₄ cups) mineral water
— 8 g dried nettles
— 14.25 g (¹/₂ oz) citric acid
— 5.4 g tartaric acid

EQUIPMENT
— Large and small scales
— Measuring pitcher
— Pan
— Induction heater
— Brix meter
— 100-micron Superbag
— Glass bottle

9.

WATERS
& MILKS

●

Flavored waters and milks are a fantastic way of introducing very soft, long, and delicate flavors into drinks. Simple, minimal, and effective. The milks are at their best for twenty-four hours; waters will keep for up to three days in sealed glass bottles.

Almond Milk

Yield: 220 ml (7¹/₂ oz)

1. In a jug, mix the *pasta di mandorle* with the mineral water.

2. Pour the liquid into a Thermomix and purée.

3. Strain using a Superbag.

Note:

If you're making this for use in the Almond Ramos recipe (page 40), you will need to measure it in grams, as specified. However, the yield produced here will be enough.

INGREDIENTS
— 62 g (2¹/₄ oz) *pasta di mandorle* (almond paste)
— 240 g (8¹/₂ oz) mineral water

EQUIPMENT
— Small scales
— Jug
— Thermomix
— 100-micron Superbag

Almond Milk Rice Water

Yield: 800 ml (3¹/₂ cups)

1. In a Thermomix, combine the mineral water with the rice and almond paste.

2. Purée until liquid.

3. Strain using a Superbag.

4. Add the cedarwood essence with a micropipette.

INGREDIENTS
— 700 ml (3 cups) mineral water
— 200 g (7 oz) sticky Japanese rice
— 30 g (1 oz) *pasta di mandorle* (almond paste)
— 50 microliters of cedarwood essence

EQUIPMENT
— Thermomix
— Measuring pitcher
— Large scales
— 100-micron Superbag
— Micropipette

Tuberose Honey Water

Yield: 400 ml (1 ³/₄ cups)

1. Weigh the honey and mix in a jug with the warm mineral water until fully dissolved.

2. Add the tuberose hydrosol with a micropipette.

INGREDIENTS
— 200 g (7 oz) Tasmanian honey
— 200 g (7 oz) warm mineral water
— 2 g tuberose hydrosol (for more information see page 107)

EQUIPMENT
— Large scales
— Jug
— Micropipette

Silver Needle Tea

Yield: 700 ml (3 cups)

1. Heat the mineral water in a pan over an induction heater until it reaches 80°C (176°F) exactly.

2. Add the tea and let it brew for 7 minutes, then strain through a fine sieve.

3. Take off the heat and add the cassis bud tincture.

4. Allow to cool before bottling.

INGREDIENTS
— 700 ml (3 cups) mineral water
— 6 g white silver needle tea
— 700 microliters of cassis bud tincture

EQUIPMENT
— Measuring pitcher
— Pan
— Induction heater
— Thermometer
— Micropipette
— Glass bottle

Olive Water

Yield: 700 ml (3 cups)

1. Put the whole olives into the centrifuge containers. Seal and spin at 4500 rpm for 10 minutes. Do this three times.

2. After each cycle (spin), drain the olive water and reseal the centrifuge containers.

INGREDIENTS
— 3.5 kg (7³/₄ pounds) green olives

EQUIPMENT
— Large scales
— Centrifuge

Olive Water

10.
DISTILLATIONS

Distillations are the ultimate bespoke ingredient to use
in a cocktail. They can make the most of entirely natural
ingredients, accommodating a wide band of flavors that
respect the original ingredient and avoid any artificial
flavorings. Flavors can be made to spec and with a specific
drink or concept in mind rather than building a concept
around an available product. Once you have the formula, it's
very easy to execute and replicate, and the results are head
and shoulders above what you can buy commercially. I've
made my own distillations that work not only in my bar but
also as a stand-alone product.

Horseradish Vodka

Yield: 1 liter (4 1/4 cups)

1. Combine the horseradish and celery root in a Thermomix and blend until the mixture is fine.

2. Mix with 700 ml (3 cups) of the vodka and pour through a funnel into the Rotavapor flask.

3. Set up the Rotavapor and gradually lower the m-bars until it reaches 35.

4. Leave to distill until 500 ml (2 cups) of liquid has been achieved.

5. Using the refractometer, rectify the ABV content to 40 with mineral water.

6. Combine 500 ml (2 cups) of the horseradish vodka with the remaining 500 ml (2 cups) of vodka.

INGREDIENTS
— 50 g (1 3/4 oz) fresh
  horseradish
— 25 g (1 oz) celery root
— 1.2 liters (5 cups) vodka
— Mineral water, to adjust

EQUIPMENT
— Large scales
— Thermomix
— Measuring pitcher
— Funnel
— Rotavapor
— Refractometer

Parsley Vodka

Yield: 500 ml+ (2 cups+)

1. Pick the parsley leaves from the stalks and add the leaves to the Rotavapor flask.

2. Pour the vodka through a funnel into the Rotavapor flask.

3. Set up the Rotavapor and gradually lower the m-bars until it reaches 35.

4. Leave to distill until 500 ml (2 cups) of liquid has been achieved.

5. Using the refractometer, rectify the ABV content to 40 with mineral water.

INGREDIENTS
— 100 g (3 1/2 oz) fresh
  flat-leaf parsley
— 700 ml (3 cups) vodka
— Mineral water, to adjust

EQUIPMENT
— Large scales
— Rotavapor
— Measuring pitcher
— Funnel
— Refractometer

Pink Peppercorn Vodka

Yield: 300 ml (1¹/₄ cups)

1. Bruise the peppercorns with a pestle and mortar and put into the Rotavapor flask.

2. Pour the vodka through a funnel into the flask.

3. Set up the Rotavapor and gradually lower the m-bars until it reaches 35.

4. Leave to distill until 300 ml (1¹/₄ cups) of liquid has been achieved.

5. Using the refractometer, rectify the ABV content to 40 with mineral water.

INGREDIENTS
— 100 g (3¹/₂ oz) whole organic pink peppercorns
— 400 ml (1³/₄ cups) vodka
— Mineral water, to adjust

EQUIPMENT
— Large scales
— Pestle and mortar
— Measuring pitcher
— Funnel
— Rotavapor
— Refractometer

Port Reduction

Yield: 250 ml (1 cup)

1. Pour the port through a funnel into the Rotavapor flask.

2. Set up the Rotavapor and gradually lower the m-bars until it reaches 35.

3. Leave to distill until 250 ml (1 cup) of liquid has been achieved.

4. Discard the 500 ml (2 cups) of clear liquid and bottle the remaining port reduction.

INGREDIENTS
— 750 ml (3¹/₄ cups) ruby port

EQUIPMENT
— Measuring pitcher
— Funnel
— Rotavapor
— Glass bottle

Pink Peppercorns in Rotavapor Flask

11.

LIQUEURS & SYRUPS

I first started making my own syrups in 1999 so that I could have a whole array of flavors at my fingertips that weren't commercially available at the time. Once I started experimenting with recipes, I found that I could produce more intense and fresher flavors. Depending on the particular cocktail in which they were used, I could go on to modify the syrup according to the drink.

Later advances in technology made the syrups more accurate, more efficient, and faster to make than ever before. It was then that I began to apply the same processes to making my own liqueurs. It's very important that you get the same Brix reading (sugar level) for each batch of syrup or bottle of liqueur (see page 160). Both the homemade syrups and liqueurs have a more natural and wider band of flavor, with no artificial flavorings or colorings. They're the perfect bespoke ingredient to pack an extra punch in any drink.

Orgeat (Almond Syrup)

Yield: 2.2 liters (9¼ cups)

1. Put the almonds in a Thermomix and blend until they become powder.

2. Combine the powder in a mixing bowl with the mineral water and orange blossom water and leave to sit for 2 hours, stirring occasionally.

3. Using a Superbag, strain the almond mix into a pan in order to separate the pulp from the water. Discard the pulp.

4. Add the sugar to the pan of almond water and, on a low heat (level 3 for an induction heater), stir until the sugar has dissolved.

5. Homogenize for 30 seconds at full power.

6. Bottle and store in the fridge.

Storage

Once opened, use within a week. Unopened, this will keep for up to 3 weeks if sealed and kept in the fridge.

INGREDIENTS
— 1 kg (2 pounds 3 oz) plain almonds
— 1.6 liters (6¾ cups) mineral water
— 10 ml (2 tsp) orange blossom water
— 1.4 kg (3 pounds) superfine baker's sugar

EQUIPMENT:
— Large scales
— Thermomix
— Mixing bowl
— Measuring spoons
— Jug
— 250-micron Superbag
— Pan
— Induction heater
— Homogenizer
— Glass bottles

Licorice Syrup

Yield: 1 liter (4¼ cups)

1. In a pan, combine the licorice powder and mineral water, mix well, and then add the sugar.

2. Heat on an induction heater at level 4 for 10 minutes. Remove the scum as it forms.

3. Once all the sugar is dissolved, bottle and leave to cool.

Storage

Once opened, use within a week. Unopened, this will keep for up to 3 weeks if sealed and kept in the fridge.

INGREDIENTS
— 40 g (1½ oz) licorice powder
— 500 ml (2 cups) mineral water
— 750 g (1 pound 10 oz) superfine baker's sugar

EQUIPMENT:
— Pan
— Large scales
— Measuring pitcher
— Induction heater
— Glass bottles

Raspberry & Violet Syrup

Yield: 700 ml (3 cups)

1. In a mixing bowl, dissolve the violet essence in the pure alcohol.

2. Add the mix to the bottle of raspberry syrup. Seal and keep refrigerated. Use within 1 week.

INGREDIENTS
— 7 microliters of violet essence
— 2 g pure alcohol
— 700 ml (24 oz) bottle of raspberry syrup

EQUIPMENT
— Mixing bowl
— Small scales
— Micropipette

Mallow Syrup

Yield: 600 ml (2¹/₂ cups)

1. Scrape the seeds from the vanilla pod into a bowl and discard the pod.

2. Combine all the ingredients in a vacuum bag and seal in the vacuum machine.

3. Cook sous vide in a bain-marie for 30 minutes at 60°C (140°F).

4. Strain using a Superbag. Use within 1 week.

INGREDIENTS
— 1 vanilla pod
— 25 g (1 oz) mallow root
— 400 ml (1³/₄ cups) mineral water
— 400 g (14 oz) sugar

EQUIPMENT
— Knife
— Large scales
— Measuring pitcher
— Vacuum machine and bag
— Bain-marie
— 100-micron Superbag

Homemade Amaretto

Yield: 700 ml (3 cups)

1. Crush the amaretti and steep in vodka for 2 days.

2. Combine the amaretti mixture in a pan with the sugar. Place on the induction heater over very low heat until the sugar has dissolved.

3. Strain through a Superbag, then bottle.

INGREDIENTS
— 200 g (7 oz) amaretti
— 500 ml (2 cups) vodka
— 120 g (4¼ oz) sugar

EQUIPMENT
— Large scales
— Measuring jug
— Pan
— Induction heater
— 100-micron Superbag

Rose Vodka

Yield: 600 ml (2¹/₂ cups)

1. Combine all the ingredients in a mixing bowl.

2. Stir to dissolve, then bottle.

INGREDIENTS
— 500 ml (2 cups) vodka
— 5 ml (1 tsp) Arabica rose water
— 200 g (7 oz) superfine baker's sugar
— 2 ml (¹/₂ tsp) tuberose hydrosol (for more information see page 107)

EQUIPMENT
— Measuring spoons and pitcher
— Large scales
— Mixing bowl

Homemade Grenadine

Yield: 1.5 liters (6¹/₃ cups)

1. Combine the pomegranate juice and sugar in a pan.

2. Heat on the induction heater at level 4 for 10 minutes. Stir continuously.

3. Allow to cool, then bottle.

Storage

Once opened, use within a week. Unopened, this will keep for up to 3 weeks if sealed and kept in the fridge.

INGREDIENTS
— 1 liter (4¹/₄ cups) fresh organic pomegranate juice
— 1.45 kg (3¹/₄ pounds) sugar

EQUIPMENT
— Measuring jug
— Large scales
— Pan
— Induction heater
— Glass bottle

Rhubarb Liqueur

Yield: 1.5 liters (6¹/₃ cups)

1. In a pan on the induction heater, dissolve the sugar in the rhubarb juice over low heat.

2. Add the vodka and malic and tartaric acids and stir.

3. Add the rose hydrosol, then bottle.

INGREDIENTS
— 500 g (1 pound 2 oz) sugar
— 480 g (17 oz) rhubarb juice
— 1 kg (2 pounds 3 oz) vodka
— 10 g (¹/₃ oz) malic acid
— 4.4 g tartaric acid
— 1 g tube rose hydrosol (for more information see page 107)

EQUIPMENT
— Pan
— Induction heater
— Large and small scales

Salted Caramel Liqueur

Yield: 300 ml (10 oz)

1. In a pan on an induction heater, make the caramel by combining the sugar and mineral water. Heat on level 10 at 170°C (338°F) for 12 minutes.

2. Take off the heat and add the salt and malic acid. Stir.

3. Add to a Thermomix and set at 50°C (122°F).

4. Mix on power 2 for 15 minutes.

5. Add the vodka and allow the liqueur to cool completely.

Storage

Once opened, the liqueur will last for 4 weeks if kept refrigerated. Unopened, the liqueur will keep for up to 2 months in the fridge. If unsure, check the aroma—the liqueur will cease to smell once it is past its best.

INGREDIENTS
— 250 g (8 3/4 oz) sugar
— 10 ml (2 tsp) mineral water
— 2.5 g Mexican salt
— 1 g malic acid
— 250 g (8 3/4 oz) vodka

EQUIPMENT
— Pan
— Induction heater
— Small scales
— Measuring spoon
— Thermomix
— Thermometer

12.
TINCTURES &
ESSENCES

Tinctures and essences are small in volume but huge in flavor. They work on the principle of reduction; by simply combining any ingredient in a high volume of liquid and then reducing it down, it becomes highly concentrated and expands inside the liquid before it disperses. When you add that to a drink the flavors reanimate and enlarge, emitting a more dense, concentrated, and powerful flavor. Essences are incredibly subtle and are a fantastic way to carry beautiful, esoteric flavors within a drink. Very high food-grade essential oils provide the base of these essences; the purer they are, the better, and the easier they are to blend. These essential oils allow me to access flavors that would be near impossible to make myself. The result is a clean mixture of ingredients that echoes the methods of perfumers for a truly unique ingredient.

It is really important if you are going to use food-grade essences that all the information about food safety and proportions is diligently read. If stored in cool, dry place in tightly sealed apothecary bottles, tinctures and essences will last for up to a year.

Tinctures

Dry Essence Tincture

Yield: 75 g (2¹/₂ oz)

1. Combine both ingredients in a mixing bowl, transfer into a sealed container, and leave for 2 weeks.

2. Set up a Rotavapor, add the mixture, and gradually lower the m-bars until it reaches 35.

3. Distill until you have reduced the liquid to 50 percent.

4. Strain with a Superbag.

INGREDIENTS
— 150 g (5¹/₄ oz) pure alcohol
— 16 capsules of grape-seed extract

EQUIPMENT
— Large scales
— Mixing bowl
— Rotavapor
— 100-micron Superbag

Pepper Tincture

Yield: 100 ml (3¹/₂ oz)

1. Blend the black peppercorns in a Thermomix until they become a fine powder.

2. Combine the pepper and pure alcohol in a glass jar.

3. Seal the jar and leave to rest for 2 weeks.

4. Set up a Rotavapor, add the mixture, and gradually lower the m-bars until it reaches 35.

5. Distill until the liquid has reduced by half.

6. Strain with a Superbag (page 220).

INGREDIENTS
— 500 g (1 pound 2 oz) black peppercorns
— 1 liter (4¹/₄ cups) pure alcohol

EQUIPMENT
— Large scales
— Thermomix
— Measuring pitcher
— Glass jar
— Rotavapor
— 100-micron Superbag

Rose Garden Aromatics

Yield: 10 g+

1. Place the 10 g of pure alcohol into an antique aromatics jar.

2. Add the oils and essences one by one using the pipette.

3. Seal the jar and gently shake to mix.

4. Leave for 6 weeks.

Comments and notes:

It is very important that the jar is sterilized and that the measurements are exact. Change the nozzle for each different oil.

INGREDIENTS
— 10 g pure alcohol
— 25 microliters of Bulgarian rose otto
— 6 microliters of Egyptian jasmine
— 8 microliters of ambrette seed
— 7 microliters of blackcurrant bud
— 6 microliters of sandalwood oil
— 3 microliters of dry essence tincture (page 186)
— 2 microliters of patchouli
— 2 microliters of cedar
— 2 microliters of cedarwood oil

EQUIPMENT
— Small scales
— Antique aromatics jar
— Micropipette

Cassis Bud Leaf Tincture

Yield: 50 ml (1²/₃ oz)

1. Combine both ingredients in a mixing bowl.

Comments and notes:

700 microns of this tincture is added to a 700 ml (24 oz) bottle of Silver Needle tea for use in the Silver Mountain (page 136).

INGREDIENTS
— 0.1 g cassis bud leaf
— 50 ml (1²/₃ oz) pure alcohol

EQUIPMENT
— Small scales
— Measuring pitcher
— Mixing bowl
— Micropipette

Gunpowder Tincture

Yield: 100 g (3¹/₂ oz)

1. Combine both ingredients in a vacuum bag, seal, and cook sous vide in a bain-marie at 60°C (140°F) for 30 minutes.

2. Remove and strain through a Superbag.

INGREDIENTS
— 8 g gunpowder tea pellets
— 100 g (3¹/₂ oz) pure alcohol

EQUIPMENT
— Vacuum machine and bag
— Bain-marie
— 100-micron Superbag

Cassis Bud Leaf Tincture

Koln Aromatics

Yield: 20 g+ (³/₄ oz+)

1. Put the pure alcohol into a jar.

2. Add the oils and essences one by one using the pipette.

3. Seal the jar and gently shake to mix.

4. Leave for 3 weeks.

Comments and notes:

It is very important that the jar is sterilized and that the measurements are exact. Change the nozzle for every new oil or essence used. Based on a tincture in Jerry Thomas's *Bartender's Guide*, 2nd edition.

INGREDIENTS
— 20 g (³/₄ oz) pure alcohol
— 21 microliters of bitter orange oil
— 2 microliters of neroli oil
— 6 microliters of petit grain oil
— 3 microliters of rosemary essence
— 63 microliters of rose water
— 2 microliters of sandalwood oil
— 20 microliters of lemon essence

EQUIPMENT
— Small scales
— Antique aromatics jar
— Micropipette

Lime Essence

Yield: 25 g (1 oz)

1. Place the pure alcohol into a jar and add the essence with a micropipette.

2. Screw on the lid and shake to mix.

INGREDIENTS
— 25 g (1 oz) pure alcohol
— 500 microliters of food-grade lime oil

EQUIPMENT
— Small scales
— Glass jar
— Micropipette

Almond Essence

Yield: 250 g (8³/₄ oz)

1. Put the skinned almonds into a microjuicer with an oil attachment, which will separate the pulp and oil.

2. Keep the oil and add the alcohol to it.

INGREDIENTS
— 250 g (8³/₄ oz) skinned almonds
— 40 g (1¹/₃ oz) pure alcohol

EQUIPMENT
— Large and small scales
— Microjuicer

Almond Blossom Essence

Yield: 40 g (1¹/₃ oz)

1. Put the pure alcohol in a mixing bowl and add the essences and oils one by one using a micropipette.

INGREDIENTS
— 40 g (1¹/₃ oz) pure alcohol
— 50 microliters of bitter almond oil
— 2 microliters of galbanum
— 2 microliters of ambrettolide

EQUIPMENT
— Small scales
— Mixing bowl
— Micropipette

Homemade Grapefruit Bitters

Yield: 600 g *(21 oz)*

1. In a mixing bowl, combine all the ingredients except the pure alcohol.

2. Blend in a Thermomix in 100g batches, for 1 minute at a time on full power.

3. Once all the batches have been blended, combine in a vacuum bag, add the pure alcohol, and seal.

4. Cook sous vide in a bain-marie at 60°C (140°F) for 30 minutes.

5. Use a Superbag to squeeze out all the excess liquid, then bottle.

Ingredients
— 75 g Sencha tea powder
— 7 g ground sandalwood
— 100 g raisins
— 60 g pink grapefruit zest
— 38 g pink grapefruit flesh
— 38 g bitter orange essence
— 60 g galanga root, grated
— 20 g orris root, grated
— 5 g quassia bark chips
— 2 vanilla pods
— 25 g cinnamon sticks, grated
— 0.2 g powdered tannins
— 3 g ground cloves
— 25 g lemon zest
— 19 g ground ginger
— 10 g ground cardamom
— 10 g ground nutmeg
— 25 g homemade burnt caramel (page 209)
— 100 g mineral water
— 50 g pure alcohol

Equipment
— Large and small scales
— Mixing bowl
— Thermomix
— Vacuum machine and bag
— Bain-marie
— 100-micron Superbag

13.
FOAMS

195 / Chamomile Foam

It was the chef Bruno Loubet who first prompted me to spark a correspondence with Ferran Adrià, asking questions about his ideas and cocktail making. This communication was to become, in essence, what stimulated me to scratch beneath the surface of what a cocktail was and could be. The subsequent correspondence built over the years has enabled me to understand his original techniques, but also to create new ones, some using the simple basics of science and others far more complex.

When I journeyed to Spain and the infamous El Bulli in 2004, Adrià was incredibly forthcoming, showing me his cocktail recipes: his open and transparent mentality was really refreshing. It was interesting to apprehend drink making at such an extremely high level through the lens of a chef rather than a bartender.

Foams were first conceived in 1998, when Adrià began working with cocktails and textures, and his creations struck me as both interesting and accessible. Foams are pure innovative pleasure. They combine both a new

texture for the senses and a new way to deliver flavor—
exaggerating but never exploiting it. It's hard not to love
the theatrical element—when the drink is taken out, heads
inevitability turn.

The basic recipe to create a foam uses gelatin and egg white
as holding agents. The emulsion is transformed into a foam
by charging it with gas in an ISI siphon. Carbon dioxide
amplifies the notes put in the canister; small bubbles burst
when drunk and release flavor. Once it leaves the siphon,
the gelatin gels into a soft web that holds the bubbles from
the gas.

I didn't want to replicate Adrià's methods exactly, but rather
translate them from the kitchen to the bar. My criteria
for creating a foam were ambitious; it had to be delicate,
beautiful to look at, and smooth and silky when consumed.
I wanted the foam to enhance the drink but keep its balance
and contrast with the liquid below it. The two layers had to
work in tandem.

An inevitable fact of creating foams for a cocktail is that the
alcohol content affects the stability of the foam. I needed
the foam to sit on the cocktail for the ten minutes it usually
takes for a cocktail to be consumed, and I wanted to ensure
that when the foam did finally disintegrate, it didn't leave
a sticky mess on the glass. The protein, which works in
gelatin to stabilize the bubbles in the foam, is attacked by
the alcohol from underneath. To reconcile this I tested the
pH level of the drink with a pH meter in order to regulate
the cocktail's acidity. If the acid content is too high it
breaks down the protein chains of the foam. I then used a
refractometer to see how strong the alcohol was when in the
actual cocktail.

With these findings I experimented with different gelatins,
trying many variations in order to find the right consistency
to keep the structure of the foam in place. Consequently,
I removed the egg white entirely and replaced it with
powdered egg white, which was not flavorful but worked
better as a bonding agent. It also makes sure that the foam
shrinks down the glass as it is drunk, leaving no mess
behind.

Chamomile Foam

Yield: 925g (1 pound)

1. Combine the mineral water with the gelatin, chamomile, vanilla, and gomme in a ceramic mixing bowl and gently stir.

2. Cover with plastic wrap and heat on low for 2 minutes in a microwave.

3. Add the powdered egg white to the mix and use an immersion blender to blend until a consistent texture is achieved.

4. Use a sieve and funnel to strain the mixture into a siphon.

5. Add the nitrous oxide charger, shake, and then chill in the fridge for an hour.

INGREDIENTS
— 800 ml (3$^1/_3$ cups) mineral water
— 3 gelatin sheets
— 30 g (1 oz) chamomile powder
— 5 ml (1 tsp) vanilla extract
— 75 ml (2$^1/_2$ oz) gomme syrup
— 15 g ($^1/_2$ oz) powdered egg white
— 1 N₂O gas charger

EQUIPMENT
— Measuring pitcher
— Small scales
— Ceramic mixing bowl
— Plastic wrap
— Microwave
— Immersion blender
— Sieve
— Funnel
— Siphon

14.

MACERATIONS

●

A maceration is when the particles of an ingredient are softened or broken up using alcohol in order to release flavor and aroma. Although this works along the same principles as cooking sous vide, macerations can sometimes be preferable because it can be difficult to release the essential oils of an ingredient at high temperatures.

White Truffle Vermouth

Yield: 700 ml (3 cups)

1. Finely chop the white truffle.

2. Add to the dry vermouth and put in a sterilized, dry glass bottle.

3. Seal the bottle with tape and leave to steep for at least 2 weeks.

Comments and notes:

The longer the mix is left to steep, the more dramatic the result. You can use this bottle as a solera system, topping it off with additional vermouth as needed, for at least 2 months.

INGREDIENTS
— 1 g white truffle
— 700 ml (3 cups) dry vermouth

EQUIPMENT
— Small scales
— Knife
— Chopping board
— Measuring pitcher
— Glass bottle

Black Truffle Vermouth

Yield: 700 ml (3 cups)

1. Finely chop the black truffle.

2. Add to the dry vermouth and put in a clean, dry glass bottle.

3. Seal the bottle with tape and leave to steep for at least 2 weeks, but ideally up to 3 months.

Comments and notes:

The longer the mix is left to steep, the more dramatic the result. You can use this bottle as a solera system, topping it off with additional vermouth as needed, for at least 2 months.

INGREDIENTS
— 2 g black truffle
— 700 ml (3 cups) dry vermouth

EQUIPMENT
— Small scales
— Knife
— Chopping board
— Measuring pitcher
— Glass bottle

15.
SOUS VIDE ALCOHOL

———————————————————————————————————•

Grapefruit Gin

Yield: 500 ml (2 cups)

1. Slice the grapefruit flesh and zest, ensuring all residual pith is removed.

2. Add all the ingredients to a vacuum bag and seal using the vacuum machine.

3. Put in a bain-marie at 60°C (140°F) for 1 hour, then remove and chill.

4. Filter the mix using a Superbag.

5. Put in the centrifuge for 10 minutes at maximum speed (5000 rpm).

6. Filter again and bottle.

INGREDIENTS
— 200 g (7 oz) grapefruit flesh
— 4 x 3 cm (1-inch) pieces of grapefruit zest
— 500 ml (2 cups) gin

EQUIPMENT
— Small scales
— Chopping board
— Knife
— Measuring pitcher
— Vacuum machine and bag
— Bain-marie
— 100-micron Superbag
— Centrifuge
— Glass bottle

Blood Orange Gin

Yield: *500 ml (2 cups)*

1. Slice the blood orange flesh and zest, ensuring all residual pith is removed.

2. Add all the ingredients to a vacuum bag and seal using the vacuum machine.

3. Put in a bain-marie at 60°C (140°F) for 1 hour, then remove and chill.

4. Filter the mix using a Superbag.

5. Put in the centrifuge for 10 minutes at maximum speed (5000 rpm).

6. Filter again and bottle.

INGREDIENTS
— 200 g (7 oz) blood orange flesh
— 4 x 3 cm (1-inch) pieces of blood orange zest
— 500 ml (2 cups) gin

EQUIPMENT
— Small scales
— Chopping board
— Knife
— Measuring pitcher
— Vacuum machine and bag
— Bain-marie
— 100-micron Superbag
— Centrifuge
— Glass bottle

Bitter Lemon Gin

Yield: 700 ml (3 cups)

1. Slice the lemon flesh and zest, retaining the pith.

2. Add all the ingredients to a vacuum bag and seal using the vacuum machine.

3. Put in a bain-marie at 60°C (140°F) for 1 hour, then remove and chill.

4. Filter the mix using a Superbag.

5. Put in the centrifuge for 10 minutes at maximum speed (5000 rpm).

6. Filter again and bottle.

INGREDIENTS
— 200 g (7 oz) lemon flesh
— 5 x 3 cm (1-inch) pieces of lemon zest
— 700 ml (3 cups) gin

EQUIPMENT
— Small scales
— Chopping board
— Knife
— Measuring pitcher
— Vacuum machine and bag
— Bain-marie
— 100-micron Superbag
— Centrifuge
— Glass bottle

Raspberry Gin

Yield: 700 ml (3 cups)

1. Put all the ingredients in a vacuum bag and seal using the vacuum machine.

2. Put in a bain-marie at 52°C (125°F) for 1 hour, then remove and chill.

3. Filter the mix using a Superbag.

4. Put in the centrifuge for 10 minutes at maximum speed (5000 rpm).

5. Filter again and bottle.

INGREDIENTS
— 700 ml (3 cups) gin
— 250 g (8³/₄ oz) fresh raspberries
— 10 ml (2 tsp) sugar syrup

EQUIPMENT
— Measuring pitcher
— Small scales
— Vacuum machine and bag
— Bain-marie
— 100-micron Superbag
— Centrifuge
— Glass bottle

Basil Gin

Yield: 200 ml (³/₄ cup)

1. Add both ingredients to a vacuum bag and seal using the vacuum machine.

2. Put in a bain-marie at 52°C (125°F) for 1 hour, then remove and chill.

3. Filter the mix using a Superbag and then bottle.

INGREDIENTS
— 200 ml (³/₄ cup) gin
— 2 g fresh basil

EQUIPMENT
— Measuring pitcher
— Small scales
— Vacuum machine and bag
— Bain-marie
— 100-micron Superbag
— Glass bottle

Shiso Dry Vermouth

Yield: 200 ml (³/₄ cup)

1. Add both ingredients to a vacuum bag and seal using the vacuum machine.

2. Put in a bain-marie at 52°C (125°F) for 1 hour, then remove and chill.

3. Filter the mix using a Superbag and then bottle.

INGREDIENTS
— 200 ml (³/₄ cup) dry vermouth
— 2 g fresh shiso

EQUIPMENT
— Measuring pitcher
— Small scales
— Vacuum machine and bag
— Bain-marie
— 100-micron Superbag
— Glass bottle

Seaweed Vodka

Yield: 500 ml (2 cups)

1. Wash the seaweed.

2. Add both ingredients to a vacuum bag and seal using the vacuum machine.

3. Put in a bain-marie at 52°C (125°F) for 20 minutes, then remove and chill.

4. Filter the mix using a Superbag and then bottle.

INGREDIENTS
— 100 g (3¹/₂ oz) seaweed
— 500 ml (2 cups) vodka

EQUIPMENT
— Large scales
— Vacuum machine and bag
— Bain-marie
— 100-micron Superbag
— Glass bottle

Wild Strawberry & Neroli Purée

Yield: *550 g (20 oz)*

1. Put the strawberries in a vacuum bag and seal using the vacuum machine.

2. Cook sous vide in the bain-marie at 60°C (140°F) for 2 hours, then remove and chill.

3. Combine the strawberries with the rest of the ingredients in a mixing bowl.

4. Pass the final mix through a microjuicer to the make the purée.

5. Homogenize the purée until it has a fine consistency.

INGREDIENTS
— 500 g (1 pound 2 oz) strawberries
— 50 ml (1²/₃ oz) fresh lemon juice
— 18 drops of Arabica orange blossom water
— 12 microliters of neroli

EQUIPMENT
— Large and small scales
— Vacuum machine and bag
— Bain-marie
— Mixing bowl
— Measuring pitcher
— Micropipette
— Transfer pipette
— Microjuicer
— Homogenizer

Pumpkin Purée

Yield: *700 g (25 oz)*

1. Peel the pumpkin with a sharp knife and chop into 2.5 cm (1-inch) chunks.

2. Seal in a vacuum bag and cook sous vide in a bain-marie at 60°C (140°F) for 2 hours, then remove and chill.

3. Pass the mix through a microjuicer to make the purée.

4. Homogenize the purée until it has a fine consistency.

5. Add the remaining ingredients and mix.

INGREDIENTS
— 500 g (1 pound 2 oz) pumpkin
— 200 g (7 oz) sugar
— 0.5 g ground nutmeg

EQUIPMENT
— Large and small scales
— Knife
— Chopping board
— Measuring pitcher
— Vacuum machine and bag
— Bain-marie
— Microjuicer
— Homogenizer

Cherry Blossom & Almond Purée

Yield: 580 g (20 oz)

1. Put the cherries and cherry blossom liqueur in a vacuum bag and seal using the vacuum machine.

2. Cook sous vide in a bain-marie at 60°C (140°F) for 2 hours, then remove and chill.

3. Pass the final mix through a microjuicer to the make the purée.

4. Homogenize the purée until it has a fine consistency, then stir in the almond essence.

INGREDIENTS
— 500 g (1 pound 2 oz) pitted fresh cherries
— 75 g ($2^2/_3$ oz) cherry blossom liqueur
— 5 g almond essence

EQUIPMENT
— Large and small scales
— Vacuum machine and bag
— Bain-marie
— Mixing bowl
— Microjuicer
— Homogenizer

Pear & Green Tea Purée

Yield: 500 g (18 oz)

1. Peel and core the pears.

2. Seal in a vacuum bag and cook sous vide in a bain-marie at 70°C (158°F) for 2 hours, then remove and chill.

3. Add the matcha and pass the final mix through a microjuicer to the make the purée.

4. Homogenize the purée until it has a fine consistency.

INGREDIENTS
— 500 g (1 pound 2 oz) Bartlett pears
— 2 g high-quality matcha green tea powder

EQUIPMENT
— Large and small scales
— Vacuum machine and bag
— Bain-marie
— Mixing bowl
— Measuring pitcher
— Microjuicer
— Homogenizer

Hot Pepper Sauce

Final Yield: 1.5 liters (6¹/₃ cups)

Part 1: Chile mix without wood

1. Chop the chiles and mix in a bowl with the salt and vinegar.

2. Add to a vacuum bag, seal using a vacuum machine, and cook in a bain-marie at 40°C (104°F) for 2 hours.

3. Remove the bag of chile mix from the bain-marie and place in a bowl of cold water until cool.

4. Empty the chile mix from the bag and put through the microjuicer. Repeat several times.

5. Strain through a Superbag.

INGREDIENTS
— 150 g (5¹/₄ oz) red chiles
— 150 g (5¹/₄ oz) green chiles
— 10 g (¹/₃ oz) salt
— 100 ml (3¹/₃ oz) malt vinegar

EQUIPMENT
— Small scales
— Knife
— Chopping board
— Mixing bowl
— Measuring pitcher
— Vacuum machine and bag
— Bain-marie
— Microjuicer
— 100-micron Superbag

Part 2: Chile mix with wood

1. Chop the chiles and mix in a bowl with the salt, vinegar, and oak chips.

2. Add to a vacuum bag, seal with a vacuum machine, and cook in a bain-marie at 40°C (104°F) for 6 hours.

3. Remove the bag from the bain-marie and place in a bowl of cold water until cool.

4. Leave for 2 days.

5. Empty the chile mix from the bag and put through the microjuicer. Repeat several times.

6. Strain through a Superbag.

INGREDIENTS
— 1.2 kg (2 pounds 10 oz) red chiles
— 1.2 kg (2 pounds 10 oz) green chiles
— 75 g (2¹/₂ oz) salt
— 450 ml (2 cups) malt vinegar
— 120 g (4¹/₄ oz) oak chips

EQUIPMENT
— Large and small scales
— Knife
— Chopping board
— Mixing bowl
— Measuring pitcher
— Vacuum machine and bag
— Bain-marie
— Microjuicer
— 100-micron Superbag

Part 3: The final mix

1. Measure the ingredients and combine in a mixing bowl.

2. Strain through the Superbag.

3. Repeat until all solid residues have disappeared.

4. Bottle.

INGREDIENTS
— 232 ml (7³/₄ oz) chile
   mix without wood
— 1.64 liters (7 cups) chile
   mix with wood
— 75 g (2¹/₂ oz) salt
— 450 ml (2 cups) malt
   vinegar
— 120 g (4¹/₄ oz) oak chips

EQUIPMENT
— Measuring pitcher
— Mixing bowl
— 100-micron Superbag
— Glass bottle

16.
MISCELLANEOUS

Just as in the English language there are irregular verbs, the language of drinks produces its own oddities: ingredients that don't quite seem to fit in. This chapter houses ingredients and techniques that work very differently from the rest.

Homemade Lemon Sorbet

Yield: 500 ml (17 oz)

1. Heat the mineral water in a pan on an induction heater and add the sugar.

2. Simmer and stir until the sugar has dissolved, then add the lemon juice and grated zest.

3. Continue to simmer and stir for several minutes and then take off the heat.

4. Once cool, strain through a Superbag into a shallow container.

5. Beat the egg whites with a whisk and fold into the mix.

6. Place in a freezer for up to 3–4 days before use.

INGREDIENTS
— 180 ml ($^3/_4$ cup) mineral water
— 240 ml (1 cup) sugar syrup
— 120 ml ($^1/_2$ cup) fresh lemon juice
— Grated zest of 1 lemon
— 2 fresh egg whites

EQUIPMENT
— Measuring pitcher
— Pan
— Induction heater
— 100-micron Superbag
— Shallow container
— Mixing bowl
— Whisk

Burnt Caramel

Yield: 160 g (5$^1/_2$ oz)

1. Heat the sugar and water in a pan on an induction heater, on level 10 or at 170°C (338°F), for 12 minutes, stirring constantly.

2. Remove from the heat and stir in the malic acid.

3. Store in an airtight plastic container in a cool, dry place for up to 4 weeks.

INGREDIENTS
— 250 g (8$^3/_4$ oz) sugar
— 10 ml (2 tsp) mineral water
— 1 g malic acid

EQUIPMENT
— Large and small scales
— Measuring pitcher
— Pan
— Induction heater

Gooseberry Gin

Yield: 700 ml (3 cups)

1. Combine the gooseberries and gin in a vacuum bag and seal using the vacuum machine.

2. Cook in a bain-marie at 52°C (125°F) for 40 minutes, then remove and chill.

3. Filter the mix using a Superbag.

4. Put in the centrifuge for 10 minutes at maximum speed (5000 rpm).

5. Filter again and bottle.

INGREDIENTS
— 150 g (5^1/$_4$ oz) fresh gooseberries
— 700 ml (3 cups) gin

EQUIPMENT
— Large scales
— Measuring pitcher
— Vacuum machine and bag
— Bain-marie
— Superbag
— Centrifuge
— Glass bottle

Green Tea Incense

Yield: 25 individual incense cones

1. Mix the powders and juniper oil together in a bowl and slowly add water, stirring gently with a spatula, until a clay-like paste has been achieved.

2. Transfer the paste into the conical molds and place in a dehydrator at 40°C (104°F) for 24 hours.

3. Remove the incense cones from the mold and cook for a further 24 hours in the dehydrator.

4. Store in a sealed shallow container, away from any moisture, for up to 1 year.

INGREDIENTS
— 100 g (3^1/$_2$ oz) makko powder
— 25 g (^{7}/$_8$ oz) cedar wood powder
— 20 g (^{3}/$_4$ oz) sandalwood powder
— 10 g (^{3}/$_8$ oz) powdered green tea
— 2 g cassia powder
— 100 microliters juniper oil
— Approx. 25 g (^{7}/$_8$ oz) mineral water

EQUIPMENT
— Mixing bowl
— Spatula
— Conical silicone molds
— Dehydrator
— Shallow container with lid

Bobbing Apples

1. Using a melon baller, scoop 25 apple balls.

2. Place them in an open tray inside a vacuum machine, which will suck the juice and air out of them.

3. Mix the mineral water with the pectin, fructose, sorbic and malic acids, and cIS-3-Hexenal.

4. Reflood the vacuum chamber with the modified juice to create the bobbing apples.

Notes and comments:

If you have any of the liquid mix left over, it will last for 1 week.

INGREDIENTS
— 2 Pink Lady apples
— 200 ml (6³/₄ oz) mineral water
— 25 g (⁷/₈ oz) pectin
— 25 g (⁷/₈ oz) fructose
— 5 ml (1 tsp) sorbic acid
— 3 g malic acid
— 100 microliters of cIS-3-Hexenal (grass essence)

EQUIPMENT
— Melon baller
— Vacuum machine
— Measuring pitcher
— Measuring spoon
— Small scales

Homemade Lipstick

1. Grate the beeswax and carnauba wax.

2. Melt the waxes together in a double boiler (or in a heatproof bowl set over a pan of boiling water), and once fully melted add the jojoba oil and castor oil to them.

3. In a separate bowl, mix the colors together well, eliminating all lumps.

4. Add the color to the wax mixture in the double boiler and let the components infuse thoroughly.

5. Once the mixture begins to cool and thicken, pour it into a small, shallow container.

6. Put in the fridge to solidify.

7. When ready to use, roll the lipstick out onto a plastic sheet ready for using the lip-shaped rubber stamp (see the Lipstick Rose recipe, page 104).

FOR THE LIPSTICK
— 25 g ($^7/_8$ oz) beeswax
— 50 g ($1^3/_4$ oz) carnauba wax
— 2 g jojoba oil
— 5 g castor oil

FOR THE COLOR
— 5 g brilliant-red food-grade powder
— 8 g deep-red food-grade powder
— 1 g violet food-grade powder
— 1 g titanium-white food-grade powder

EQUIPMENT
— Grater
— Heatproof bowl
— Mixing bowl
— Pan
— Small scales
— Induction heater
— Shallow container
— Acetate plastic sheet
— Rolling pin
— Lip-shaped rubber stamp

Homemade Lipstick Ingredients

17.
GLASSWARE

Drinking is a sensual pleasure, and the glass in which you deliver a drink can make or break the enjoyment factor of its contents. Aesthetics and the perception of taste are interwoven; the visual aspect of the glass is very important, and a fine martini glass will produce an entirely different aura when drinking a Martini than a mass-produced mold will. Drinks do taste different in different glassware: the weight, texture, thickness, raw material, and shape are all factors in the taste experience.

Years spent working in bars and serving the same style of drink in different glassware have led to this collection of my favourite styles, and the majority of the recipes in this book have been made with a particular glass in mind.

Small Coupette

Yield: 3.5 oz

I have always felt that stirred drinks should be made in small quantities and consumed in three or four sips, ensuring that a drink stays perfectly cold right until the last drop. These 3.5 oz coupettes are perfect; a large Martini that takes forever to drink will inevitability end up warm, and a warm Martini is pure blasphemy.

Large Coupette

Yield: 7.5 oz

To serve shaken drinks, I favor these coupettes over a more traditional martini glass or goblet. They have a pleasant aesthetic curve that is particularly practical for drinking sours, the foam of which requires a large surface area so as not to dissipate quickly.

Highball

Yield: 11.25 oz

My preferred highballs are reminiscent of glassware used in Italian cafés. More elegant than most styles available, the narrow glass allows the ice cubes to stack on top of one another.

Rocks Glass

Yield: 4.5 oz

For me, a good rocks glass is a simple style of tumbler that has clean, modern curves. Neither fancy nor ornate, the glass should never distract from the drink. I've found that glasses that are 4.5 oz are the perfect size to fill to the brim with ice so that it looks ready to pop out of the glass.

Champagne Flute

The champagne flute has been somewhat neglected of late in favor of serving champagne in coupettes. Champagne looks and feels more decadent sipped from a coupette, but there are scientific reasons why any drink with bubbles tastes better in a flute. A champagne flute has a smaller surface area and this concentrates the bubbles and the aroma upward and toward your nose. The larger the surface area, the more the bubbles break and the more the aroma is lost as the alcohol volatiles escape and come into contact with the air.

Riedel Grappa Glass

This glass is great for controlling the way in which you inhale the aroma of a drink. Its slight convex lip allows aromatized champagnes to release their aromas just as they reach your nose. This glass is perfect for The Rose (see page 110), the aromatics of which would become trapped and therefore too intense if delivered in a traditional champagne flute.

Sake Glass

Yield: 1 to 1²/₃ oz

The sake glass is a small cylindrical vessel traditionally used in Japan for the serving of sake. They are designed to hold between 1 oz and 1²/₃ oz and are perfect for sipping from.

Bibliography

Adrià, Ferran, Albert Adrià, and Julie Solier. *El Bulli: 1998–2002.* Spain: ARA Libres, 2002.

Aftel, Mandy. *Essence & Alchemy: A Book of Perfume.* London: Bloomsbury Publishing, 2001.

Baudelaire, Charles. *The Flowers of Evil.* New York: Oxford University Press, 1998.

Blumenthal, Heston. *The Big Fat Duck Cookbook.* London: Bloomsbury Publishing, 2008.

Burr, Chandler. *The Emperor of Scent.* London: Arrow Books, 2004.

Degroff, Dale. *The Essential Cocktail: The Art of Mixing Perfect Drinks.* New York: Clarkson Potter, 2009.

De Mente, Lafayette Boye. *Kata: The Key to Understanding & Dealing with the Japanese.* Tokyo: Tuttle Publishing, 2003.

Dornenburg, Andrew, and Karen Page. *Culinary Artistry.* New York: John Wiley & Sons Inc., 1996.

Embury, David. *The Fine Art of Mixing Drinks.* 1st ed. New York: Doubleday, 1948.

Gagnaire, Pierre. *Reflections on Culinary Artistry.* New York: Stewart, Tabori & Chang, 2003.

Grieve, Maude. *A Modern Herbal.* London: Penguin, 1977.

Hemphill, Ian. *The Spice and Herb Bible: A Cook's Guide.* Australia: Pan Macmillan, 2000.

Johnson, Harry. *Bartender's Manual: Mixellany Commemorative Edition.* London: Mixellany Limited, 2009.

Jones, Andrew. *The Aperitif Companion: A Connoisseur's Guide to the World of Aperitifs.* New York: Knickerbocker Press, 1998.

LaVey, Szandor Anton. *The Devil's Notebook.* San Francisco: Feral House, 1992.

Meier, Frank. *The Artistry of Mixing Drinks.* Paris: Fryam Press, 1936.

McGee, Harold. *On Food and Cooking.* New York: Scribner, 1984.

Plato. *The Republic*. London: Penguin, 2003.

This, Hervé, and Pierre Gagnaire. *Cooking: The Quintessential Art*. Berkeley: University of California Press, 2008.

Thomas, Jerry. *The Bartender's Guide: How to Mix Drinks*. 2nd ed. New York: Dick & Fitzgerald, 1862.

Turin, Luca. *The Secret of Scent: Adventures in Perfume and the Science of Smell*. London: Faber and Faber, 2006.

Turin, Luca, and Tania Sanchez. *Perfumes: The A–Z Guide*. New York: Penguin, 2009.

Wondrich, David. *Imbibe! From Absinthe Cocktail to Whiskey Smash, A Salute in Stories*. New York: Perigee Books, 2007.

Wondrich, David. *Punch: The Delights and Dangers of the Flowing Bowl*. New York: Perigee Books, 2010.

Glossary

Affila sprig Part of the cress family, an attractive-looking vegetable that has a mild nutty taste.

Agar-agar A gelling agent derived from seaweed that retains its gelling properties up to a temperature of 80°C (176°F).

Angelica An earthy, bittersweet herb with a flavor reminiscent of juniper.

Bruising Similar to muddling but more gentle.

Building To construct a drink over ice directly inside the glass in which it is served rather than in a shaker or cocktail tin.

Cassia bark A tropical evergreen tree, the bark of which (when ground) has a flavor akin to cinnamon but with a more bitter aftertaste.

Cassis bud The bud of the blackcurrant plant. It has an earthy, sulphuric, and mineral taste.

Clarify The act of making a liquid clear.

Dewar flask A thermal container in which to keep liquid nitrogen safely.

Dry shaking Shaking drinks without ice. This is a binding method that allows the protein chains of the egg white to stretch more, giving you a better foam on top of the final drink.

Flash cotton A piece of cotton soaked in a dry, flammable nitrocellulose liquid. When lit, the cotton completely disappears with a magical puff.

Florence fennel Part of the fennel family, this aromatic herb has a mild anise-like flavor with a sweet aftertaste.

Heads and tails The result of any distillation is divided into three separate parts in the following order: heads, hearts, and tails. The best and desired portion of the distillation is obtained from the hearts. Cut-off points have to be determined between heads, hearts, and tails—the art lies in judging when to start collecting the hearts and when to stop.

Homogenize The act of breaking up the fibers of an ingredient (see also page 158).

Hydrosol A water-based essence that suspends essential oils inside water through the process of distillation.

Hyssop A small, bushy aromatic plant of the mint family with distinct, bitter leaves.

Juniper A spicy, flowery herb with a pine-like, resinous taste.

Makko A Japanese binding agent made from the bark of evergreen trees, native to Southeast Asia.

Melissa An aromatic herb also known as lemon balm.

Micropipette A pipette that measures in microliters ($1/1000$ of a millileter). They are invaluable for measuring incredibly small amounts of liquid accurately (see also page 158).

Nootkatone A natural organic compound and aromatic of grapefruit.

Orris root A spice derived from irises grown in the eastern Mediterranean region, with a distinct floral, yet bitter, taste with an aroma of violets.

Quassia bark The bark of a bitter herb indigenous to South America.

Rinsing a glass The action of pouring a liquid over ice in a glass, swirling the liquid with a bar spoon, and then discarding both liquid and ice. This leaves a subtle hint of flavor and aroma on the glass.

Ruscus An evergreen shrub with attractive but flavorless inedible leaves.

Salivating mix A liquid that increases the amount of saliva produced in the mouth.

Shochu A clear, distilled Japanese spirit, usually made from sweet potato or rice.

Siphon A utensil originally designed to whip cream and used in modern professional kitchens for the making of foams.

Sous vide Cooking ingredients with the use of a vacuum machine and bain-marie (see also page 148).

Sugar syrup All recipes using sugar syrup have been made with 2 parts cane syrup to 1 part water.

Sugaring/salting the rim of a glass The action of moistening the rim of the glass with a slice of citrus fruit and running the rim over a plate of sugar or salt.

Superbag A very fine mesh bag through which liquids can be strained and clarified.

Transfer pipette A piece of equipment used to transport a measured volume of liquid.

Tuberose A root from the same family as the agave plant with essential oils that are traditionally used in perfume.

Twist A small piece of peel with the pith removed, twisted over a drink in order to release the oil. It is then usually dropped in a drink as a garnish. If the recipe calls for the twist to be discarded, twist the zest over the drink but do not use as a garnish.

Vetiver grass A grass mostly found in Africa, it has a fresh, woody scent. Its oil has real staying power on the skin and is often used in perfumes.

Volatiles Molecules that easily evaporate at normal temperatures and pressures.

Xanthan gum A product derived from fermented starch, used as a thickening agent and to maintain solids in suspension within a liquid.

Index

222

Acknowledgments

Adam "there's a rumour" Peters-Ennis, Addie "Chin" Chinn & Sarianne Plaisant, Alessandro "la minchia" Boneschi, Andreas "the dude" Tsanos, Arthur "gin shots!" Combe, Bayode & Claire "it's a wicked suit" Oduwole, Ben "speedo" Reed, Ben "beautiful" Williams, Cami "it was your shoe love" Hobby-Limon, Cara "you dumb ass" Soronen, Cas "it's a Korean" Oh, Chad "lonestar" Solomon, Charles "pint of sake" Vexenat, Claudio "el niño" Antonio, Dale "back in the 1860's" Degroff & Jill "sit still!" Degroff, Dave "otarded" Arnold, Dave "the bar dent" Wondrich, Desmond "I've seen something like this before" Payne, Don "these are some of my favourite things" Lee, Eric "don't leave the room" Fossard, Flavio "bin 364!" Clementi, Fab "who were those guys?" Limon, Frances "I'm his Mum" McKevitt, Gary "breathe in, breathe out" Regan, Guillaume "living the dream" Le Dorner, Giacamo "si professor" Russo, Giles "well, you know" Gavin-Cowen, Hobby "helllloooo" Limon, Ian "more chile" Morgan, Ingrid "it's done" Gordon, Jack "I've got ice on my head" Robertiello, Jake "this is how you throw a dart" Burger, Jared & Anastasia "you're naughty" Brown & Miller, Jeff "did she just do that" Morgenthaler, Jenifer "no ice! no fooking fruit!" Griffin, John "barf" Gakuru, Jim "you're all slaves" Wood, Junior "jun the trooper" Romeo, James "Jocky" Petrie, Kay "Peter!" Dorelli, Kim "Gargamel doesn't exist" Ireland, Kenta "hangover press-ups" Goto, Louisa "am I drunk?" Gavin-Cowen, Luc "the cardboard box" Merlet, Maria "Tonyeee you're late!" Ballester, Marcis "Byron" Dzelzainis, Meimi "what bicycle" Sanchez, Melissa "Chewbacca" Goodman, Marco "I invented you something" Arrigo, Micky & Sammy "what shall we wear today?" McIlroy-Ross, Magga "is it a man?" Kristjansdottir, Mal "you know who that is" Evans, Nick "it has to be the 45" Strangeway, Oliver "do what you want" Peyton, Paul "dirty" Weldon, Harold "deliciousness" McGee, Peter "Rolling Stones" Dorrelli, Richie & Amanda "I gotta tell you something" Boccato, Sean "darkside" Harrison, Shawn "kismey" Kelley, Simon "red wine" Knight, Simon "the stunt double" Conigliaro, Simon "why the **** is it on top of the door" Ford, Stuart "lap of glory" Bale, Steve "I got something" Olson, Stuart "go on" Ekins, Sandrae Lawrence & Gary Sharpen "oh go on then," Spike "you are so pooky" Merchant, Stuart "my head hurts" Tilley, Thoma "it's cool" Girard, Tom "the difference between" Whitehead, Wayne "edamame" Collins, Zoe "I just blushed" Burgess.

To all the wonderful customers, employers, and colleagues I have met on this journey and the teams at 69 Colebrooke Row and the Zetter Townhouse for putting up with some off-the-beaten track ideas . . . Anybody I have forgotten, please accept my most sincere apologies . . .